PROSPER WITHOUT COMPROMISE

Faith, Strategy, and the Inner Alignment That Sustains Abundance

Kevin Adou

Published by Alignment Press
www.alignmentpress.com

ISBN: 979-8-9949216-0-9

DEDICATION

To all who seek to build with integrity,
to prosper with purpose,
and to walk in abundance
without losing their soul.

TABLE OF CONTENTS

INTRODUCTION

THE BUILDER'S AWAKENING

There are two kinds of success. One fills bank accounts but leaves the heart empty. The other fills the heart—and, in time, often fills the accounts as well.

Why do some people, despite status, money, or recognition, live in constant tension, fragmentation, or dissatisfaction? And why do others, facing equally demanding circumstances, move forward with peace, clarity, and fruitfulness—as if their success followed a more just and ordered design?

What truly makes the difference? This book was born from that question.

It does not offer another method to stack on top of the ones you already know. It invites a shift in posture: from survival to creation, from dispersion to alignment, from anxious control to conscious cooperation with deeper laws—spiritual, human, and universal. This path sometimes requires profound inner realignment, because no lasting structure can be built unless the source is first clarified and restored to order.

The Source Before the Strategy

Everything begins in a place often overlooked: the inner life. Before the first action, before the plan, before the strategy, there is an invisible impulse that shapes everything that follows: intention.

Intention is the inner pilot. It quietly influences your decisions, the way you perceive opportunities, your relationship to work, and even the quality of what you attract. When the source is clear, the flow is clear. When the heart is aligned, action becomes naturally fruitful.

We have perfected our tools but often lost touch with the source. Yet no external success can sustainably compensate for inner disorder. The kind of abundance that brings peace and endures always flows from the inside out.

Abundance Through Alignment: The Movement of the Four Pillars

Peaceful and lasting prosperity is generated from within. To make this tangible, I have structured this journey around a coherent and powerful movement—an alliance of four stages that transforms an invisible idea into concrete reality:

1. Intention (to intend). Everything begins with the purification of the source. This is the act of deciding from the heart—of deliberately choosing a direction no longer driven by fear or lack, but by deep alignment with your calling. Here, intention does not refer to emotional desire but to a conscious inner decision: the act of setting direction before energy, strategy, or action follows. In this sense, intention becomes the pilot of your destiny.

2. Strategy (to plan). An intention without a path remains a dream. This stage gives form to your vision. By structuring long- and short-term objectives (through the DAP framework and AMT goals), you chart the road ahead. Planning is not rigid control but the design of the channel through which abundance can flow.

3. Faith (to believe). This is the emotional and spiritual engine. Once the plan is drawn, faith is what animates it. It is the discipline of attention that refuses to feed doubt and instead focuses on the certainty of the promise. To believe is to inhabit your future before it manifests.

4. Action (to embody). This is the final seal. Action is the signal sent to heaven that you are ready to receive. By embodying your convictions through consistent, concrete steps, you move from theory to harvest. Action is the visible proof that faith is alive.

But how do we turn invisible intention into clear direction? How do we ensure that what we seek to build is aligned with our true nature rather than shaped by external pressure?

Intention is the fuel, but vision is the engine. And for that engine to run smoothly, it needs a frame of reference. This is where a compass I call the DAP Vision comes into play: a three-dimensional framework that tests the purity and solidity of your projects before the first stone is ever laid.

Seeing Before Building: The DAP Vision

After intention comes vision—but not just any vision. A grounded, coherent, and fruitful vision, structured in this book around a simple compass: **DAP — Desire, Love, and Potential.**

- **Desire:** the inner fire that sets you in motion.
- **Love:** what purifies ambition and directs it toward service and impact.

- **Potential:** what you already carry within you—talents, skills, experiences, and resources.

When these three dimensions align, vision ceases to be an abstract dream. It becomes a clear heading, an embodied mission capable of attracting the right decisions, the right encounters, and the right resources.

Abundance as Flow, Not Stock

The world teaches us to accumulate in order to feel secure. Biblical wisdom teaches us that abundance circulates.

Abundance is not a stock to defend but a flow to allow. It expands in proportion to responsibility, generosity, and the capacity to become a source. The more you allow it to circulate, the wider the channel becomes.

Why This Book, and Why Now

If these words resonate with you, it is no accident. Perhaps you feel the call to succeed without losing yourself, to build without hardening your heart, to prosper without sacrificing your peace.

This is a transformational book—designed not only to inspire you, but to catalyze real and lasting change. It is meant to guide you from Point A (confusion, stagnation, inner blockage) to Point B (clarity, alignment, and decisive action).

It offers a step-by-step journey, intentionally moving you from inner alignment to outward embodiment. Throughout the book, you will find reflective exercises, practical frameworks, and guided orientations to support your growth.

Scripture quotations are drawn from the Holy Bible. The prayers included may be spoken as written or adapted to your own voice and spiritual sensitivity. What matters most is not repetition, but resonance—that the words become yours, lived and internalized.

This journey requires your full ownership. Transformation happens not by reading alone, but by engagement—by allowing the principles to shape your thinking, your posture, and your daily choices.

This book will help you:

- clarify and purify your intention;
- cultivate attention that turns faith into conviction;
- take concrete and fruitful action;
- build aligned professional and financial projects;
- unite meaning, performance, and responsibility.

At the end of this journey, you will not simply be more competent. You will be aligned. Aligned with your heart. Aligned with your calling. Aligned with your peace.

Turn the Page

You are entering the path of the conscious builder—one who creates, invests, works, and decides in alignment with who they truly are. When heart, mind, and action move together, coincidences become providence, and the ground is prepared before you can even see it.

You are ready.

Ready to build.

Ready to receive.

Ready to manifest.

Turn the page.

The journey begins now.

We will first explore the power of your intention (Chapter 1), before shaping your strategy (Chapters 2–4), strengthening your faith (Chapter 5), and finally moving into action (Chapter 6).

CHAPTER 1

INTENTION: THE SOURCE BEFORE STRATEGY

Introduction: The Invisible Decision That Precedes All Creation

Everything begins within. Before the first action, before strategy, even before a clearly articulated vision, there is an invisible impulse: intention. It determines the direction and quality of everything we build. Like an inner pilot, it guides each decision, attracts certain opportunities, deflects others, and quietly shapes our reality.

In a world obsessed with methods, tools, and results, we often forget a fundamental principle: we never harvest beyond the nature of the seed we plant in our hearts. And the heart is precisely that hidden place where intentions are formed—pure or confused, inspired or self-centered—which eventually become visible actions.

The laws of the Kingdom rest on this mystery: everything begins with intention, and the quality of that intention determines the quality of what follows.

Before seeking the right strategy, God invites us to examine the right source. Before "doing," He teaches us how to "be." Before running after results, He calls us to align the heart.

This chapter is therefore the first stone of the structure that will lead you from intention to abundance. We will not yet speak of techniques or action plans but of the very source of creative power—that conscious and spiritual energy placed within you to transform intention and inner drive into reality.

Together, we will explore how a clear, pure, and Kingdom-aligned intention becomes the invisible force that opens doors, attracts favor, and makes possible what may seem impossible. For true intention is an inner decision—a silent alliance between your will and divine grace.

1.1. "Let There Be Light"—And There Was Light

All creation—divine or human—begins with intention. Nothing lasting is born by accident. Behind every work, every enterprise, every life transformation, there is first an inner decision.

When the Creator speaks those powerful words, "Let there be light," He releases a pure intention, carrying a clear direction and creative power capable of shaping the universe. This statement establishes a foundational principle: before any visible manifestation, there is a conscious and aligned will. God does not react—He creates. And each time we act with a clear and consecrated intention, we participate in that same creative principle.

In human life, this process repeats itself at every scale and in every area of success:

- Before the creation of a business blessed by God, there is an inner decision—a sincere desire to serve with integrity, to create value and employment, and to become a source of blessing through entrepreneurship.

- Before the publication of a book that positively transforms lives, there is the inner decision to release a message that can no longer remain contained.
- Before a meaningful gift that changes a life, there is an intention of generosity that overcomes the fear of personal lack.

That spark—that decision—is intention.

1.2. The Heart: The Inner Altar, Source and Control Center

Everything we manifest externally—success, relationships, peace, or abundance—takes root in an invisible seed: the intention of the heart. What your heart consistently feeds, your life eventually reveals and expresses.

- If your heart is driven by fear, envy, or the need for recognition, those energies will sooner or later shape your outcomes.
- But if your heart is inhabited by faith, peace, love, and a sincere desire to fulfill God's will, that inner light will be reflected in your decisions, your balance, and the quality of your success.

"Above all else, guard your heart, for everything you do flows from it." — Proverbs 4:23

The heart is the source of life in the deepest sense. It determines the nature of the river you release into the world. It must be guarded, protected, and purified—because if the water is troubled at the source, the river of your life will be troubled as well.

You likely turned to this book because you desire to manifest abundance in your life—material and financial abundance lived in peace. Yet what sustainably nourishes your resources while preserving your peace always begins with what dwells in your heart.

We often spend our lives searching for the key to success in the external world: degrees, strategies, networks, or opportunities. But the true law that governs lasting elevation—the one that does not age and does not depend on seasons or circumstances—is not found outside. It is internal. It is within you. It begins in the heart, that sacred place where intentions, directions, and blessings are formed.

What this book calls *Prosper Without Compromise* begins with a pure intention and a heart aligned with the divine perspective of abundance. In other words, if your intention is to manifest prosperity while preserving inner peace, the very first step is to position your heart to receive and live abundance according to God's design.

Allow me to illustrate this with two contrasting forms of success:

- **Apparent success, prosperity, and abundance**—admired by the world, yet often leaving the soul empty.
- **Approved success, prosperity, and abundance**—validated by God, carrying peace, balance, joy, and protection.

This book is meant to guide you toward the second: a form of success that honors God because it flows from a pure heart and a righteous intention. The divine perspective on abundance positions you as a channel, not the source—allowing the abundance and peace that come from God Himself to flow through you.

1.3. Becoming the Source: Abundance as Divine Flow

In the world, we are taught early on to accumulate in order to become wealthy. In the Kingdom, we learn to give in order to become fruitful.

"Give, and it will be given to you… For with the measure you use, it will be measured back to you." — Luke 6:38

This statement is not merely a moral exhortation; it reveals a spiritual law. From a divine perspective, abundance is never a fixed stock hoarded out of fear of lack. It is a living flow—a continuous movement that passes through those who agree to become its channel. Abundance is not preserved; it is transmitted. It does not stagnate; it flows. And the more it circulates, the more it expands.

If you desire an abundance that honors God—including material and financial abundance—the primary question is not how much you possess but who you choose to be. Choose to be a channel connected to the Source—one through whom the flow of abundance passes in order to bless others.

Abundance and prosperity begin to manifest in your life the moment you position yourself as a channel rather than a reservoir. In the Kingdom's logic, abundance does not respond to need; it responds to seed. God multiplies what you give, not what you withhold. If you see yourself as someone who lacks, you will reflect that condition. But if you see yourself as one who has enough to give to those in need, Heaven recognizes you as such—and entrusts you with more, so that you may continue to be a vessel of divine abundance.

1.4. The Clash of Laws: Two Logics, Two Destinies

Throughout our lives, two opposing logics quietly confront one another in the hidden places of our hearts.

The Law of the World vs. the Law of the Kingdom

- **The world's logic:** "Hold on in order to have." It closes the hand, feeds the fear of lack, and traps the soul in constant vigilance. The more one withholds, the more one fears losing. This is the path of stagnation.
- **The Kingdom's logic:** "Give in order to receive." It opens the hand, releases trust, and establishes deep peace. The more one shares, the stronger the current becomes. This is the path of movement.

Choose the logic of the Kingdom. You are not a reservoir meant to be filled and then drained; you are a channel. The moment you withhold, the flow contracts. The moment you allow it to pass through you, it expands. The abundance that preserves your peace is the natural consequence of spiritual alignment—not the reward for exhausting struggle. It manifests to sustain your capacity to give, serve, and bless.

Poverty Mindset vs. Abundance Mindset

Two additional logics confront each other within our thoughts:

- **The poverty mindset:** It fixates on lack, debt, and anxiety about tomorrow. It leads to constant self-pity and verbalizes limitations repeatedly. By continually speaking of material constraints, one programs the subconscious with lack. Over time, the individual identifies with deprivation, unknowingly prophesying scarcity over their own life and conditioning themselves to remain there.

- **The abundance mindset:** It does not deny difficulties but refuses to give them center stage. It focuses attention on what is already present and available to bless the world—even in the midst of hardship. It gives thanks for what is already there and gives with joy, trusting God as the sole Source and Provider.

Choose the second: the abundance mindset. Where the first programs the subconscious for survival, the second programs it for life. By identifying with the Source rather than with circumstances, you begin to speak abundance over your life. Heaven then recognizes you as a faithful steward and entrusts you with more—so that you may continue to be an instrument of divine generosity.

1.5. God: Your Only Source and Your Faithful Provider

Choosing the logic of the Kingdom and the abundance mindset is not merely an intellectual exercise; it is a radical act of faith that requires genuine surrender.

Take a moment to examine the state of your soul. What occupies your thoughts right now? Do you feel that tightening in your chest—that weight carried by anxiety about tomorrow? If your heart is filled with fear or stress regarding finances, it is a sign that you are still carrying this burden alone, on your own shoulders. But today, an invitation is extended to you.

Lay Your Burden at the Foot of the Cross

Transformation begins the moment you accept that you are no longer meant to be your own source of security. Jesus opens His arms to you:

"Come to me, all who labor and are heavy laden, and I will give you rest." — Matthew 11:28

Laying your burden at the foot of the Cross means entrusting your bills, your debts, and your unmet needs to the One who has already accomplished everything. It is accepting that your current circumstances do not define your future provision.

Reconnect with the Father's Faithfulness

Why doubt His ability to care for you? Christ invites us to observe creation to understand the heart of God:

"Look at the birds of the air: they neither sow nor reap nor gather into barns, and yet your heavenly Father feeds them. Are you not of more value than they?" — Matthew 6:26

If God clothes the lilies of the field with a beauty surpassing that of Solomon, how much more will He care for you. Your role is not to exhaust yourself in worry, for:

"Which of you by worrying can add a single hour to his life?" — Matthew 6:27

Your role is to restore God to the center:

"Seek first the kingdom of God and His righteousness, and all these things will be added to you." — Matthew 6:33

Peace as Compass and Guardian of the Heart

The sign that you have truly entered the process of surrender is the arrival of a new peace. The apostle Paul gives us the complete key in Philippians 4:6–7:

"Do not be anxious about anything, but in everything, by prayer and supplication with thanksgiving, let your requests be made known to God. And the peace of God, which surpasses all understanding, will guard your hearts and your minds in Christ Jesus."

Why is this peace the key?

It surpasses understanding.

The peace God gives is not logical. Human reasoning says peace comes only when bills are paid and accounts are full. Kingdom peace is supernatural—it settles in while the storm is still raging. It does not depend on circumstances but on connection to the Source. If you feel calm while everything seems uncertain, it is a sign that you have stopped striving in your own strength and have begun to rest in Him.

It stands guard.

The original text suggests that the peace of God "stands watch" over you. Like a soldier at the gate of a fortress, this peace filters what attempts to enter your mind. It prevents thoughts of lack, fear, and poverty mindset from crossing the threshold of your heart.

It protects both heart and mind.

The subconscious is the seat of emotions (the heart) and decisions (the mind). By entrusting your burdens to Jesus, you allow His peace to saturate both. Instead of prophesying lack, you begin to perceive opportunities and solutions that anxiety once concealed from you.

A Faith Exercise for Today

Make this choice now:

1. Identify the burden you are carrying (a debt, a stalled project, fear about the future).
2. Present it to God with thanksgiving—not thanking Him for the problem itself, but because He is already the solution.
3. Claim His peace. Simply say:

   "Lord, I place this at Your feet. I refuse to worry. I receive Your peace that guards my heart."

The moment you sense that peace settling within you, you will know the channel is open. Heaven no longer perceives you as a man or woman in distress but as a calm and trustworthy steward of divine abundance.

1.6. Positioning Yourself as a Creator-Giver

Anyone who desires to receive abundance must first choose to become its source. This posture radically transforms the way you live. You no longer see yourself as a beggar dependent on circumstances but as a creator-giver—an instrument through whom God acts. God never multiplies what you hide. He multiplies what you present.

This is one of the most consistent laws of Scripture: multiplication always begins with a visible seed—often ordinary, sometimes insignificant in human eyes.

Remember the well-known scene. Faced with a hungry crowd, the disciples, overwhelmed, focus on their small supply—"We have only five loaves and two fish"—and conclude that it is worthless, that it will never be enough. Jesus does not reason from a mindset of lack. He asks them,

"Bring them to Me." He did not ask for what they did not have; He asked for what they already had.

What was insignificant in their hands became sufficient in the hands of God. The decisive moment was distribution: multiplication did not occur during prayer but during the giving. The moment they released that "small" seed, God became the river. What seemed minimal became overflowing—twelve baskets filled.

It is always the same. Multiplication begins when you agree to give what you already have.

Abundance Begins on the Inside

True abundance is born long before it manifests externally. Your first wealth is not financial—it is internal: spiritual, emotional, and identity-based. The first thing you offer the world is not your money. It is yourself.

You already carry within you:

- your love and compassion,
- your wisdom and discernment,
- your joy, humor, and presence,
- your knowledge and talents,
- your material and financial resources,
- your network, your voice, your strength,
- and above all, the presence of God dwelling within you.

From this perspective, the principle becomes clear: if you want more of something in your life, become its source. If you want more wisdom, begin by offering wisdom. If you want more peace, sow peace. If you want to see miracles, start by embodying the miracle.

To manifest abundance—including material and financial abundance—you must first act as though abundance were already your natural state. Not by illusion but by inner alignment. Be abundant. And do what abundance would do. Even if you possess little, give from it. For when you position yourself as the source, God can only reflect and multiply what you choose to be. Abundance always comes to those who decide to be its initiators.

By giving what you have, you break the belief in lack. You open yourself as a channel through which blessing flows freely. As Saint Francis so simply expressed it: "It is in giving that we receive."

Giving with Discernment and Love

A word of caution: giving is not an empty or automatic gesture. Generosity must be a conscious act, filled with meaning and soul.

Sharing your resources—whether love, wisdom, attention, or financial means—must flow from a heart full of love and genuine care. True generosity responds to real needs.

For this act to carry depth, it requires discernment. You should not give out of obligation but out of conviction. It is vital to "sense" the act inwardly and to desire to serve sincerely—or better yet, to ask God to guide you, so that you may learn to give according to His compassionate and loving heart.

It is also essential to give toward the work of God. This is where you are invited to experience His grace and provision in a tangible way.

Consider this unique invitation:

"Bring the whole tithe into the storehouse... Test Me in this," says the Lord Almighty, *"and see if I will not open the windows of heaven and pour out for you a blessing beyond measure."* — Malachi 3:10

This is the only place in all of Scripture where God explicitly invites us to test Him—and He does so in the area of generosity. Why? Because this act touches three deep realities of your being: faith, trust, and your understanding of God as an inexhaustible Source.

This is not a tax, nor a mechanical obligation. It is a supreme act of recognition—acknowledging that everything you possess comes from Him and ultimately returns to Him. When you give to God, you are symbolically declaring:

"Lord, You are the source of my life, my resources, my opportunities, and my future."

It is an inner posture of humility, gratitude, and trust.

Understand this: everything you give with love—whether to bless others or to honor God—returns to you, amplified and multiplied in various forms—yes, including material and financial provision.

The miracle of abundance is not found in what you lack but in what you already hold in your hands. It is activated the moment you choose to give it. For when you give what you have, God gives what He has—and His supply is infinite.

This is the essence of this teaching: external abundance is never a conquest; it is the natural consequence of an inner abundance that is shared.

1.7. Articulating Intention

Choosing to live in abundance—in all its forms, including material and financial—while remaining in the peace of contentment begins with a fundamental realization: you are not meant to live as a passive receptacle, dependent on circumstances, but as a source, a channel through which blessings flow.

This inner alignment is expressed when you willingly offer your talents, passions, and resources in service to others and for the glory of God. This is not an abstract idea or a theoretical principle but a profound shift in posture—an inner awakening that transforms the way you think, decide, and act in daily life.

Positioning yourself as a source is a daily discipline. The abundance you receive is never independent of your capacity to give. Life's energy is a flow, never a stock. The more you open yourself, the stronger the current becomes. But for this intention to move beyond a mere inner feeling, it must be formulated, articulated, and presented to God. As long as it remains unspoken, it stays a dormant seed. When it is expressed in faith, it becomes a living seed—carrying direction, multiplication, and favor.

This is where many hesitate. Why tell God what He already knows? And yet, in the Gospels, Jesus asks a striking question: "What do you want Me to do for you?" When He addresses Bartimaeus, the blind man, it is not to gather information. The miracle is released at the precise moment the man articulates his intention: "Lord, I want to see."

This scene reveals a fundamental spiritual law: God acts in response to expressed intention, not because He is unaware of our desires but because He invites us to consciously enter into covenant.

Formulating your intention is an act of alignment. As long as it remains vague, your energy is scattered. The moment you declare it—through words, prayer, or writing—it takes shape. It moves from the realm of the undefined into the realm of creation. In doing so, your heart and mind jointly sign an agreement before God.

Expression clarifies your thinking, transforms a diffuse desire into a precise decision, and that clarity naturally attracts direction and provision. It fully engages you: you move from spectator to co-creator, acknowledging that your success unfolds through cooperation between your will and divine wisdom. It also anchors your faith, because you cannot actively believe in what you have not named.

A wish hopes.

Intention decides.

A wish says, "I hope this happens."

Intention says, "Lord, this is what I choose to build with You."

God does not enter into covenant with a wish but with those who make a clear inner decision. When intention is articulated, grace is set in motion. Coincidences become alignments, opportunities gain definition, and resources appear—not through agitation but through agreement with the divine current.

This is the principle of the Kingdom: ask, seek, and knock—not to inform God but to activate the law of conscious asking and become a partner in His work. An unspoken intention remains an idea. An articulated intention becomes a covenant. And an aligned intention attracts favor. This is why every intention meant to bear fruit must be expressed, presented, and entrusted to the Source—so that what you declare in faith may be confirmed by Heaven.

1.8. Defining, Formulating, and Presenting Your Intention to God: The Seal of the Covenant

After understanding the nature of intention, its creative role, and the importance of a purified heart, here comes the most decisive step: consciously articulating your intention and presenting it to God.

As long as an intention remains internal and implicit, it stays a possibility. When it is formulated with clarity and faith, it becomes a commitment. This transition—from the internal to the declared—is what seals the covenant. You are no longer merely hoping; you are choosing, positioning yourself, and cooperating.

To help you discern and articulate your intention, here are a few examples you may draw inspiration from. These are not magic formulas but guides to help you find words that align with your heart:

- *My intention is to live in an abundance that is activated as I become an open channel. I sow as the disciples shared the loaves and fish. I choose to be the source through which God can distribute, open doors, nourish, multiply, and manifest His glory in the lives of others.*
- *I am a source. I am channel of God's abundance. I live in material and financial abundance and in the peace of contentment, generously placing my talents, skills, and resources at the service of humanity and for the glory of God.*
- *I manifest a just, lasting, and abundant prosperity. My life is a living testimony of God's faithfulness, enriching, serving, and transforming others through the resources available to me and the gifts He has placed within me.*
- *My intention is to allow God to use what I give and who I am, so that He may multiply, nourish, and spread His prosperity through me.*

- *I walk in a prosperity that reflects the goodness of God, placing my talents, gifts, and resources at the service of the common good, in order to build and uplift lives for His glory.*

Practical Exercise: Clarifying Your Intention

This moment is essential. Treat it as a foundational act.

Step 1: Listening and Formulation

Take a few moments of silence.

Formulate your intention in one, two, or three simple, clear, and aligned sentences. You may draw inspiration from the examples above or write your own.

Step 2: Presenting Your Intention to God

Here is a prayer to seal your intention:

Heavenly Father,
Source of all life and all abundance,
I present to You my intention:
(read your intention aloud)

Purify it, align it with Your wisdom,
and make it a seed of just and fruitful prosperity.
I offer You what I have—
multiply it for Your glory
and make me a source of abundance,
provision, and blessing for others.

Lead me into a prosperity that is peaceful,
lasting, and aligned with Your plan.

May the fruit of my work glorify You
and bless many.

In Jesus' name.
Amen.

Before going any further in this book, an essential step is required. For all lasting prosperity begins with a restored inner order. What follows is neither a ritual nor an obligation but a foundational passage—a moment of realignment designed to purify the source before multiplication.

1.9. Restoring the Inner Altar Before Multiplication

Many people pursue abundance by focusing on multiplying strategies, prayers, and visible initiatives. Yet the kind of prosperity that honors God and preserves peace is not released through asking alone, human effort, or intellectual capacity. It is activated when spiritual foundations are restored, purified, and put back in order. Before external doors open, inner altars must be restored.

This is why every conscious builder is called to pass through three essential spiritual gateways. They are neither symbolic nor optional. They mark a decisive turning point—an inner seal that prepares lasting fruitfulness:

- **repentance**, which purifies the source;
- **spiritual authority**, which breaks restraints;
- **and the prayer of provision**, which opens the flow of abundance that comes from God.

1.9.1. The Prayer of Repentance: Restoring Order and Responsibility

In the Kingdom, prosperity is never separated from responsibility. God always entrusts before He multiplies. And everything He entrusts—time, talents, resources, opportunities, finances—calls for faithful, conscious, and aligned stewardship. Where management is disordered, multiplication is blocked; where order is restored, favor flows.

Repentance in the context of prosperity goes far beyond acknowledging a moral fault. It touches the way a person has managed what was entrusted to them. It is possible to sincerely desire abundance while living from a posture of self-sufficiency: making decisions without prayer, pursuing projects without discernment, spending without vision, or placing excessive confidence in one's own abilities. This posture creates an inner rupture. It leads to exhaustion, fragility, and limited fruitfulness.

To repent here is to acknowledge that God has not always been fully restored to the center of life's management. It is to reestablish the proper order: God as Source, human beings as stewards (Deuteronomy 8:18). Where this order is blurred, prosperity becomes unstable, fragmented, or conflicted. Where it is restored, peace returns and growth becomes secure.

This repentance involves confessing unhealthy relationships with money and resources—fear, excessive attachment, anxiety, greed, or negligence—and choosing a new posture: trusting God as Provider, refusing to worry about tomorrow, and relying on His faithfulness (Matthew 6:25–34; Philippians 4:19). It leads to a financial and material life aligned with the Kingdom: intentional generosity, support of God's work, care for those in need, wise stewardship, and discernment in opportunities.

Repentance is restoration, not condemnation. It opens the inner space where divine wisdom can once again govern, guide, and secure growth.

It prepares the ground, purifies the source, and makes the heart available for a just, peaceful, and lasting prosperity. For when alignment is restored, God opens the windows of heaven according to His order (Malachi 3:10).

Preparing Yourself for the Prayer of Repentance

Before entering this prayer, pause for a moment. Do not read these words as a formality but as an invitation. Repentance is not a religious obligation; it is a free and conscious choice of realignment.

Allow the Spirit of God to search your heart. Without fear, examine how you have managed what was entrusted to you—your time, your talents, your opportunities, and your resources. This is not about self-judgment but about truthfully recognizing what has been done without God, beside Him, or apart from Him (Psalm 139:23–24).

Approach this prayer with humility and trust. God never reveals in order to condemn but to restore. Where you acknowledge disorder, He is ready to restore order. Where you release control, He is ready to resume governance.

Simply offer a sincere heart. Whoever confesses finds mercy, and whoever turns away receives favor (Proverbs 28:13). Pray slowly and intentionally, as a foundational act. This moment marks a turning point: the purification of the source before multiplication.

When you are ready, enter now into the prayer of repentance.

Prayer of Repentance: Consecration of Resources and Dependence on God

Heavenly Father,
I come before You with a humble and sincere heart,
for nothing is hidden from Your sight.

I acknowledge that in certain seasons of my life,
I have not always honored Your wisdom
in the way I managed the resources You entrusted to me.

You gave me time, talents, relationships,
opportunities, and material means,
yet at times I acted without consulting You,
relied more on my own calculations than on Your guidance,
and sought security in my own strength
instead of fully depending on You.

I repent of every decision made without prayer,
every project pursued without alignment,
and every resource mismanaged
through haste, fear, or lack of faith.

Forgive me for forgetting
that it is You who gives the power to create wealth.

Today, I renounce all self-sufficiency
and every illusion of control apart from You.
I acknowledge that without You I can do nothing,
and that in You I am able to accomplish
what aligns with Your purpose.

Purify my heart, renew my mind,
and restore within me the spirit of a faithful steward.
I return to You the governance of my finances,
my projects, my income, and my investments.

Teach me to trust You before counting my resources,
to seek Your wisdom before activating my abilities,
and to place You at the center of all lasting prosperity.

I receive Your forgiveness, Your grace, and Your restoration,
and I choose from this day forward
to walk in humility, obedience, and trust.

In the precious name of Jesus Christ,
Amen.

Inspired by: Proverbs 3:5–6; Deuteronomy 8:18; Luke 16:10–11; John 15:5

1.9.2. The Prayer of Authority and Declaration: Breaking Chains and Releasing Divine Prosperity

Once inner order has been restored, another dimension must be activated: spiritual authority. Not everything that hinders prosperity falls automatically through repentance or good intention alone. Certain forms of resistance—cycles of debt, persistent delays, repeated blockages, abnormal stagnation—remain because they have never been explicitly confronted and broken.

In the Kingdom's logic, words are active power. Speech does not merely describe reality; it shapes it. What is tolerated internally and confirmed verbally eventually establishes itself. Conversely, what is confronted, overturned, and declared in faith is dismantled (Proverbs 18:21).

The prayer of authority is exercised in the name of Jesus Christ, clothed in the authority obtained through His sacrifice and victory. The one who prays does not speak in their own name but on the basis of a finished work. For the Son of God appeared to destroy the works of the enemy—including those that keep God's people bound in lack, fear, or bondage (1 John 3:8).

This prayer therefore targets the breaking of chains: chains of poverty, debt, chronic delay, inherited or accepted limitation. It proclaims the end of yokes that restrict fruitfulness and announces a new order aligned with the will of God (Isaiah 10:27). Where chains are broken, movement is restored.

Exercising spiritual authority does not deny visible realities; it refuses to let them have the final word. It declares that God is the Source, that He gives the power to create wealth in order to establish His covenant, and that the prosperity that comes from Him is now released (Deuteronomy 8:18). It affirms that the blessing of the Lord rests upon the household of the righteous and that abundance finds its place there (Psalm 112:3).

Without this step, a builder may carry a righteous vision within an environment that is still spiritually locked. Spiritual authority then acts as an act of governance: it removes obstacles, clears passageways, and allows divine prosperity to circulate freely, without confusion or disruption. For in the Kingdom, deliverance precedes establishment, and spiritual release prepares visible manifestation (Mark 11:23).

Preparing Yourself for the Prayer of Authority

Before entering this prayer, take a moment to position yourself inwardly in authority—not through human strength but through spiritual alignment. This prayer is not a plea; it is an act of governance. You are not speaking in your own name but in the name of Jesus Christ, clothed with the authority secured by His sacrifice and victory.

Remember that whatever binds, delays, or blocks is not inevitable. Certain chains do not fall through the mere desire for change but through conscious and declared confrontation. What you do not address remains. What you confront in faith can be broken (Mark 11:23).

Examine with clarity the areas where prosperity seems hindered: recurring cycles, persistent debt, chronic delays, and unexplained stagnation. Do not observe them with resignation but with discernment. The Son of God appeared to destroy the works of the enemy—not for you to endure them but for you to walk in the freedom He obtained (1 John 3:8).

Approach this prayer with confidence and sobriety. This is not about shouting or striving but about declaring the order of the Kingdom. Where chains are broken, movement resumes. Where authority is exercised, pathways are cleared.

When you are ready, enter now into the prayer of authority and declaration, and proclaim in faith what must be established.

Prayer of Authority: Restoring the Flow of Prosperity

Heavenly Father,
I come before You in the name of Jesus Christ,
clothed in the authority You have given me
through His sacrifice and His victory.

Your Word declares that the Son of God appeared
to destroy the works of the enemy.
Today, I stand on this truth
and exercise my spiritual authority in faith.

In the name of Jesus Christ,
I break every visible and invisible chain
that hinders my God-ordained prosperity.

I break every form of financial stagnation,
every unjustified delay,
and every inherited, learned, or accepted limitation.

I declare that every yoke is destroyed
by the anointing of the Lord.

I refuse to let lack, fear of insufficiency,
or a spirit of delay govern my life.

I cancel every negative word
spoken against my financial future.
I tear down every mental stronghold
that prevents me from fully receiving
the wealth and abundance God has prepared for me

Now, I invoke and proclaim
the abundance that comes from God alone.

I declare that closed doors are opening.
I declare that blocked paths are being cleared.
I declare that delayed seasons are aligning
with the divine timetable.

I receive the prosperity that enriches
without adding sorrow.
I receive divine favor
that accelerates without corrupting.
I receive the right resources,
legitimate opportunities,
and God-ordained connections.

I declare that I shall lack nothing,
for the Lord is my Shepherd.
I declare that I am a source and not an empty reservoir.

My financial life is now aligned
with the Kingdom of God—
His righteousness, His wisdom, and His peace.

I proclaim it in faith,
I establish it by the Word,
and I receive it with gratitude.

In the mighty name of Jesus Christ.
Amen.

Inspired by Isaiah 10:27; Luke 10:19; Deuteronomy 28:12–13; Proverbs 10:22; Psalm 23.

1.9.3. The Prayer of Provision: Receiving Abundance According to the Order of the Kingdom

After repentance, the source is purified. After authority is exercised, chains are broken and pathways are cleared. Then comes the time of provision.

The prayer of provision is not a simple request to God to fill a material lack. It is the act by which the builder fully acknowledges God as Source and consciously positions himself as a channel. It does not arise from fear, urgency, or greed but from restored inner alignment and a faith that has matured.

In the order of the Kingdom, God provides where He governs. Divine provision does not flow through disorder, haste, or spiritual independence. It manifests when the heart is aligned, when speech is right, and when intention is purified. This is an abundance that responds to posture more than to formula.

The prayer of provision rests on a foundational truth: God knows our needs before they are expressed, and He has already prepared the resources required to fulfill what aligns with His will (Matthew 6:8; Philippians 4:19). But receiving this provision requires more than verbal asking—it calls for confident faith, aligned speech, and an inner readiness to steward what will be entrusted.

Prosperity according to God is never aimed at sterile accumulation. It is given to establish, sustain, transmit, and bless. It equips the builder to fulfill his mission, care for those entrusted to him, honor commitments, and become a source for others. This is why the prayer of provision is inseparable from responsibility. God gives the power to create wealth, but He expects faithful, wise, and conscious stewardship in return (Deuteronomy 8:18; Luke 16:10).

This prayer also marks a profound shift in posture. The builder no longer sees himself as dependent on circumstances, people, or systems. He places himself under exclusive dependence on God—without passivity and without anxiety. He no longer demands in worry; he receives in trust. He no longer forces doors open; he discerns the ones God opens (Psalm 127:1).

The prayer of provision is also a prayer of peace. Divine prosperity is not accompanied by inner turmoil or moral disorder. It enriches without stealing the soul, without dulling the conscience, without diverting one from their true calling (Proverbs 10:22). It endures over time, protects inner balance, and preserves spiritual alignment.

Finally, this prayer commits the builder to becoming an active steward of what he receives. Faith that asks without action remains incomplete. Divine provision calls for concrete choices: discipline, generosity, wise management, discernment in investment, and faithfulness in small things as well as in great ones (James 2:17; 2 Corinthians 9:8–11).

Thus, the prayer of provision is neither a demand nor a magical formula. It is the expression of a lived covenant. It inwardly seals what was purified through repentance and released through authority. It opens the flow of a just, ordered, and peaceful abundance—one that comes from God and endures.

It is in this spirit—of faith, gratitude, and responsibility—that you may now enter into the prayer of provision.

Prayer to Receive Divine Provision

Eternal Father, my Provider and my Source,
You are the One who calls into existence
what does not yet exist.

You are the source of all true wealth—
the kind that does not corrupt the soul
and does not steal peace.

I thank You because You know my needs
even before I express them.
I believe that You take pleasure
in the prosperity of Your servant
when it is aligned with Your will.

I declare that You open
the storehouses of heaven over my life.

I receive wisdom to create, manage,
and multiply resources.
I receive inspired ideas, divine strategies,
and righteous partnerships.

May my work be blessed.
May my projects bear fruit.
And may I become a source of blessing to others.

I choose to seek first Your Kingdom,
and I trust that all other things
will be added unto me.

Thank You, Lord,
for I live in trust, gratitude,
and aligned abundance.

In the name of Jesus Christ.
Amen.

Inspired by: Matthew 6:33; Philippians 4:19; Deuteronomy 8:18; Psalm 23

Everything that needed to be restored on the inside has now been restored. The source has been purified, spiritual order reestablished, and dependence acknowledged. But alignment—no matter how deep—is not an end in itself. It is the starting point of conscious construction.

The next chapter marks this transition: the moment when vision takes on clear, structured, and intentional form. For God does not govern ambiguity, and lasting prosperity is always built upon a vision that is discerned, embraced, and ordered.

CHAPTER 2

BUILDING YOUR DAP VISION: DESIRE, LOVE, AND POTENTIAL

Introduction: From Intention to Vision

In the previous chapter, you took the most fundamental step: clarifying your Intention. You chose to become a channel. Remember—this inner posture is not a magic formula; it is an act of radical will. Intention calibrates your energy and aligns your heart to receive divine grace. But energy without direction inevitably leads to dispersion. This is where vision is born.

If intention is the engine, vision is the steering wheel. Vision maps your future. It is the strategic blueprint that gives clear direction to the energy of abundance you have chosen to activate. After defining who you choose to be (your intention), the most strategic question now arises: What are you going to build in order to create wealth? (your vision).

Abundance, prosperity, and lasting wealth are not abstract concepts that fall from the sky. They are the result of deliberate production and intentional action in the real world. Abundance is not wishful thinking; it is the fruit of commitment, effort, creativity, and socio-economic responsibility.

2.1. Your Strategic Battlefield: Socio-Economic Embodiment

Your vision must take form within the socio-economic sphere. This is your field of action—your strategic battlefield—where you design, build, and multiply your projects. Vision acts as the compass that directs the energy you have mobilized toward the creation of tangible value.

This contribution—essential for wealth creation—takes three primary forms.

Salaried Expertise

Salaried work should no longer be seen as simple subordination but as the structured deployment of your skills in collaboration with an employer. It is a partnership in which your expertise meets the organization's resources to generate value.

If you choose to pursue a salaried path, it is essential to understand that it is not a final destination but a structuring phase within your broader socio-economic vision. Today, employment is no longer an end in itself; it becomes a versatile tool in service of personal ambition. Beyond a monthly salary, it provides financial stability that enables you to build savings for future investments.

Choosing salaried work does not exclude plurality. By developing parallel activities or preparing future ventures while employed, you transform your current position into a continuous resource stream that supports your long-term vision.

Entrepreneurship

To undertake is to dare to build what does not yet exist. It is responding to a real need with a concrete solution. The entrepreneur transforms tension into opportunity, ideas into systems, and vision into reality. Profit is not the sole objective; entrepreneurship creates value, unlocks talent, and expands what is possible for an entire community.

Investment

To invest is to think beyond oneself. It is allowing capital to work in order to amplify vision, secure the future, and prepare for transmission. It is sowing today to harvest tomorrow—not only for oneself but for those who will come after. Investment is the expression of a mature, patient, and strategic vision.

Strategic Intelligence: Weaving a Tapestry of Abundance

Authentic vision does not operate through restriction but through orchestration. It does not rely on a single lever of action; it learns how to make multiple levers work together. In today's economy, resilience no longer comes from dependence on a single source but from the ability to combine strengths intelligently.

This is where strategic intelligence comes into play: the art of creating a coherent ecosystem in which each activity supports the others and every flow nourishes the whole. Lasting abundance is built like a tapestry—thread by thread—through continuity and balance.

Synergy is not a luxury; it is a form of protection. A vision built on a single pillar remains exposed. Diversification, on the other hand, absorbs shocks, navigates cycles, and maintains forward momentum. When one channel slows down, others sustain the movement. The trajectory remains stable even as conditions change.

This approach also creates powerful leverage. Present stability becomes a strategic resource: predictable income funds emerging projects, and secured time today purchases freedom tomorrow. Each stage of professional life ceases to stand alone and instead becomes a link in a larger construction.

Strategic intelligence also requires conscious energy management. Some activities demand direct, intense, and creative involvement; others primarily require capital and patience. Vision then acts as a conductor, harmonizing these demands without dispersion or burnout.

Different expressions of this synergy can be observed:

- the professional who uses the stability of a primary role to invest wisely;
- the entrepreneur who converts business growth into lasting wealth through a structured investment strategy;
- or the individual who simultaneously integrates security, creation, and accumulation, giving rise to a virtuous cycle of development.

These trajectories are neither accidental nor the result of overactivity. They emerge from a conscious choice: to think of one's life path as a system.

The Imperative of Clarity: Declaring Your Path

The architecture of your abundance is a personal decision. Some will choose the simplicity of a single pillar; others will embrace the disciplined complexity of diversification. Neither option is inherently superior. What makes the difference is clarity.

Where are you truly committing yourself? Through which channels do you intend to allow the abundance you are building to circulate? Whether it is a clearly embraced career direction, a structuring entrepreneurial project, or a well-defined investment strategy, vision then becomes a roadmap.

Before guiding you through the practical formulation of this vision, it is crucial to integrate two foundational principles that will provide the mental fuel and discipline required to turn your dream into reality:

1. **The Principle of Precedence:** How vision precedes provision (the archetype of Abraham).
2. **The Principle of Direction:** Why vision serves a triple role—as direction, filter, and fuel.

Understanding these principles is the key to transforming effort into effectiveness and aspiration into fulfillment.

Let us now turn to the archetype of Abraham to grasp the power of visioned sight.

2.2. The Principle of Precedence: Seeing Before Receiving

Before any strategy, before sustained effort, before discipline itself, there is a governing principle: vision precedes provision. Nothing lasting manifests without first being seen inwardly. Vision is the first embodiment of a future that does not yet exist; it is tomorrow painted on today's canvas.

Seeing is not daydreaming. To see is to make real in the mind what does not yet exist in the material world. You cannot build what you have not first contemplated with clarity, conviction, and faith. Every fruitful work begins with an inner image strong enough to guide thought, decision, and action.

Scripture reveals this principle through the foundational archetype of Abraham. God does not begin by giving him the land, nor by granting the promised child. He begins by shaping his sight.

"Lift up your eyes and look from the place where you are, northward and southward and eastward and westward; for all the land that you see I will give to you." — Genesis 13:14–15

Here, the act of seeing is a prerequisite for possession. The promise becomes active only after the vision. Abraham must first internalize what he is called to receive externally. Vision is not an abstract dream; it is a mental map—an anticipatory ownership of the future.

Confronted with a reality that contradicts every promise—an aging man, without a child, without biological prospects—God does not attempt to explain or reassure through arguments. He operates on a different level: vision. He subjects Abraham to a second, deliberately radical exercise, designed to shift his inner center of gravity.

"Look toward heaven, and number the stars, if you are able to number them… So shall your offspring be."— Genesis 15:5

With this command, God does not ask Abraham to understand, but to contemplate. He replaces the visible limits of the human condition with an image without limits—one that cannot be grasped by reasoning alone. The goal is not to inform Abraham but to reprogram his imagination, to have him mentally inhabit a reality greater than what his senses can confirm.

God anchors the impossible in Abraham's mind before inscribing it in time. The promise ceases to be an external word and becomes an internal image. And it is precisely here that faith is born—not as a passing emotion or fragile optimism, but as a stable inner certainty nourished by a vision that has been accepted and embraced.

Material provision—the land, the child, the legacy—manifests later. But it is already sealed in the vision. What you can see with faith is what you can carry with responsibility.

This law remains unchanged. Your career, your business, your future assets all obey it as well. You must learn to see the fulfilled version of your life before the resources, connections, and opportunities appear.

2.3. Your Vision: A Compass with Three Functions

If vision is the condition for provision, it is also the strategic tool that structures your daily life. A life without vision resembles a ship without a heading: much movement, little progress. You stay busy, you work hard, you exhaust yourself—and yet you drift.

Scripture is unequivocal:

"Where there is no vision, the people cast off restraint." — Proverbs 29:18

Without vision, energy scatters, priorities blur, and growth withers. Vision is your antidote to drift. It functions as a compass with three essential roles: direction, filter, and fuel.

Direction

Without vision, you react to circumstances. With vision, you choose. Vision frees you from the tyranny of urgency and sterile busyness. It becomes the inner heading that guides your daily decisions. Each action is measured against a single, decisive question: *Does what I'm doing today move me closer to who I am called to become?* Vision transforms disordered activity into intentional progress. It becomes your anchor.

Filter

A clear vision simplifies life. It acts as both a spiritual and strategic filter. It allows you to say yes without hesitation to what is aligned—and no without guilt to what diverts you, even when it appears attractive. Vision protects your time, your energy, and your focus. It reminds you of what truly matters for your future. What you refuse is as important as what you pursue.

Fuel

When fatigue sets in, when obstacles repeat themselves, when results are delayed, your vision becomes your emotional and spiritual fuel. It gives meaning to sacrifice and coherence to discipline. Vision turns discipline into passion and labor into mission. It gets you back on your feet when everything suggests giving up. With a clear vision, obstacles are no longer walls—they become steps.

You have now laid the foundation. Vision is neither a luxury nor a slogan; it is the bridge between heaven and earth, between intention and action, between faith and reality. It is time to articulate it with precision so it can become a clear, embodied, and actionable roadmap.

This is precisely the role of the DAP Vision Compass, which we are now ready to activate.

2.4. The Vision Methodology: The DAP Compass

This chapter introduces the methodological heart of this book: a strategic compass designed to balance passion, service, and talent, and to guide you through the socio-economic channel—or channels—you choose to pursue.

Dimension	Key Question	Inner Indicator
Desire	What truly sets me in motion?	Energy, joy
Love	How does this bless others?	Meaning, peace
Potential	What do I already carry to begin?	Confidence

When desire is purified by love, when love is expressed through service, and when potential is put to work, vision becomes fruitful, stable, and compelling.

God blesses what is desired with purity, served with love, and carried out with faithfulness.

The DAP framework restores harmony by helping you connect what you want to do (Desire), what you are called to do (the law of Love), and what you are able to do (Potential).

2.4.1. Desire: The Sacred Fire

Your desire is the inner star that continues to shine even when your sky grows dark. It is the first spark of every living vision—the quiet yet persistent force that pushes you to move forward, to dream, and to create, even when circumstances seem unfavorable. Without desire, there is no lasting movement; without inner fire, vision remains theoretical.

But the desire we are speaking of here is neither a whim nor a passing craving. It is not an emotional impulse dictated by trends or comparison. Authentic desire is a deep, stable passion that endures across the seasons of your life. It is what has stirred you for a long time, what repeatedly returns to your awareness even when you try to ignore it. It often bears the trace of a calling.

Scripture captures this truth with great precision:

"Delight yourself in the Lord, and He will give you the desires of your heart."
— Psalm 37:4

This verse does not promise the fulfillment of every desire, but the sanctification of those that are genuine. God does not despise your deepest aspirations. When desire is lived in communion with Him, it is purified, directed, and transformed. What might have remained a personal ambition becomes a mission filled with meaning, service, and blessing.

In this light, your professional, entrepreneurial, or financial projects cease to be merely human goals. They become channels through which God can release life, prosperity, and impact. When you build from a consecrated desire, you engage your whole being. You give the best of yourself—to your clients, your partners, to society—and that inner quality inevitably bears fruit. God does not oppose your desire; He seeks to elevate it so it becomes a source of life, for you and for others.

A Lesson from Experience

I have observed this truth closely over many years while supporting African students in their career orientation at the Jesuit University of Abidjan. When I asked them which professions or activities truly made them come alive, many responded with painful resignation: "Here, you take the job you can find, not the one you love."

Behind that sentence lay the weight of unemployment, family pressure, and—above all—the fear of dreaming. Many had come to believe that dreaming was a luxury reserved for others. They felt compelled to accept whatever came, even if it meant completely disconnecting from what deeply animated them. I understood them. In certain contexts, economic urgency can crush hope.

But I often told them this: "If you abandon your deepest desire, you risk spending half your waking life doing work that has nothing to do with your inner fire. And nothing is more exhausting than suffocating, day after day, what you carry within."

Work occupies a significant portion of our lives. When God said to Adam, "By the sweat of your brow you shall eat bread," He was not pronouncing a curse but establishing a law of fruitful effort. When that effort is invested in an activity disconnected from your inner fire, it becomes suffering. But when it is aligned with your authentic desire, it becomes a source of joy, growth, and blessing.

To dream does not mean denying reality. To dream is to refuse to be imprisoned by it. It is believing that God placed a specific desire and potential within you for a reason. Of course, everything does not manifest instantly. But when you identify what you truly love and commit your faith, discipline, and perseverance in that direction, you always move closer to it.

I have seen many former students transform their trajectories. Some dared to change direction; others stepped away from predetermined routes to pursue their true passions. Years later, I continue to see them grow—entrepreneurs, international civil servants, educators, leaders, builders. They all share one common thread: they are engaged in work that inspires them, stretches them, and creates value for others. They are not free from hardship, but they have stopped betraying their inner fire.

The lesson is simple and powerful: dreaming is allowed—even, and especially, in difficult contexts. A job you do not love drains you faster. Work aligned with your desire makes you more alive, more creative, and more fruitful. Your authentic desire is a divine seed. Do not let it be extinguished by fear or resignation. Water it with faith, courage, and love—it will bear fruit.

That is why I invite you to formulate your vision and your goals not from what you are enduring today but from what you choose to build tomorrow. Refuse to let your current circumstances define the limits of your horizon. Present limitations indicate a starting point—never a destination.

The real danger is not lack but fixation on lack. When attention remains locked on obstacles and past failures, imagination contracts and faith weaken. It is not difficulty that kills a dream but the inner abandonment of the right to dream.

So, allow yourself to think big—not out of pride but out of faithfulness to what is alive within you. A vision that requires neither faith nor growth is too small. What you dare to see with courage today prepares the paths you will walk tomorrow.

Identifying Your Authentic Desire: Recognizing the Traces of the Inner Fire

Identifying your true desire is not about inventing something new; it is about learning to read the traces left by a fire that has already been burning within you. This inner fire is not a passing emotion. It is a stable, quiet, yet persistent energy that has been orienting you for a long time.

To begin this discernment, ask yourself these simple—but demanding—questions:

- What ignites your heart even when no one is watching?
- What makes you persevere without the immediate expectation of reward?

- What, when you do it, brings life, peace, and meaning—to you and to others?

Where your fire burns without consuming your peace, you are likely walking in the direction of your calling.

This fire is unique. It carries the signature of your deepest identity. It does not always appear in dramatic or obvious ways. More often, it hides in what feels natural, almost ordinary: your spontaneous impulses, your recurring interests, what you do without being asked, what you return to again and again. God rarely speaks through noise; He often reveals Himself through consistency.

What Moves You with Joy: The Nourishing Fire (The Joy Test)

The first sign of authentic desire is revealed in what you do with joy, without constraint or calculation. These are the activities that nourish you rather than drain you—those you would continue even if no one applauded. They point to an inner zone of flow where your energy circulates naturally.

For some, this fire expresses itself through creating solutions, solving problems, or technological innovation. They find joy in coding, structuring, automating, improving. Their desire may take form through digital tools, FinTech platforms, SaaS solutions, or innovations that serve efficiency and the common good.

For others, the fire is expressed through hospitality and service: welcoming, organizing, caring for experience, pursuing relational excellence. Their desire is not merely to produce or sell but to create connection, warmth, and care. This fire may give birth to projects in hospitality, events, or lifestyle ventures.

For some, attention is drawn to cities, neighborhoods, and buildings. They see potential where others see decay. Their desire is to build, restore, structure, and provide housing. Their fire may take shape in real estate, urban development, or sustainable and social housing.

Others carry a fire of healing and empathy: relieving suffering, restoring balance, supporting inner or physical transformation. Their desire finds expression in health, wellness, care, coaching, or prevention.

What you do with joy and without constraint is rarely accidental. It is often a seed placed within you.

What Moves You, Offends You, and Endures Over Time (The Fire of Mission)

Desire is not revealed only by what you enjoy doing but also by what you can no longer tolerate seeing. Righteous indignation is often a disguised calling. What deeply wounds you in the world may indicate what you are meant to help transform.

Moses did not receive his calling during a mystical experience but when he witnessed injustice inflicted upon a slave. Nehemiah did not hear a heavenly voice; his heart broke when he learned that the walls of Jerusalem were in ruins. What breaks your heart often reveals what can be repaired through you.

Perhaps you are stirred by unequal access, glass ceilings, or economic exclusion. Your indignation may call you toward empowerment, leadership, and structural justice. Perhaps you are troubled by the exploitation of small producers, unjust value chains, waste, or environmental destruction. Your fire may then lead you toward fair, sustainable, and innovative solutions.

Another fundamental indicator is energy. True desire does not empty you—it fills you. Even when the work is demanding, you emerge more alive, more alert, more grounded. Ask yourself:

- After which activities do you feel more alive than before?
- Where do you experience a deep peace, a sense of inner rightness?
- Which tasks cause you to lose track of time?

What energizes you without consuming you often points to a zone of grace—where desire and calling intersect.

Finally, observe consistency. Authentic desire is not a trend; it is a red thread. Across the seasons of your life, it returns, sometimes in different forms. What you did for pleasure as a child may, as an adult, become a mission lived with conviction. God does not extinguish what He ignites; He waits for you to learn how to direct it consciously.

The Right to Realignment

A crucial step now emerges: defining—or redefining—your mission. Your path is never fixed; it is a living journey that becomes clearer as you move forward. Whether you are at the starting point or already well underway, you have the right—and sometimes the responsibility—to realign when what you are doing no longer fully expresses who you have become.

If You Are at the Beginning (Defining)

If you do not yet have a stable professional or economic activity, this is your greatest freedom. Begin by focusing your energy on what genuinely excites you—those activities that awaken enthusiasm, feed imagination, and make you feel fully alive. Move forward. Experiment—not in dispersion, but in attentive listening to what sets you in motion internally.

Consciously make space for your sacred fire. Allow yourself to observe it, honor it, and let it express itself without censoring it in the name of caution or fear of mistakes. This fire needs to be acknowledged. For it is within this space of assumed freedom, nourished by faith, that the purest vision is born—one that does not seek to imitate but to reveal who you are called to become.

If You Are Already on the Path (Redefining and Realigning)

If you are already engaged in a professional or economic activity but feel inner fatigue, disharmony, or disengagement, know this: the dream is still permitted. This imbalance is a signal that your heart and your work are no longer aligned.

You have two strategic options—both valid.

Creating a New Channel of Abundance (Strategic Transition)

You are free to reorient yourself, even to change direction entirely, to align with what truly fuels you. However, from a standpoint of economic wisdom, radical change is not always immediately necessary.

- **The training lever:** Reorientation or the creation of a new activity often requires new skills. Strategically pursuing additional training prepares you for a new career or equips you to launch a parallel venture (entrepreneurship or investment). Training becomes an investment in your future potential.
- **The parallel activity concept:** Your stable activity can become the patron of your dream. Use it to finance and secure the launch of a parallel activity aligned with your inner fire.
- **The evaluation strategy:** Grow this new activity quietly. Test its viability and its capacity to generate abundance. When this new

channel becomes sufficiently strong, stable, and fulfilling, it can gradually replace your original activity. This is transition built on security, not haste.

Realigning the Mission without Leaving (Inner Repositioning)

Sometimes, leaving is not required. Frustration does not come from what you do but from why you do it. In such cases, the solution is to look at the same activity from a new angle and redefine your mission from your inner fire.

- **Changing intention:** If you are an accountant, your work is no longer simply "producing reports" but bringing strategic clarity and ethical transparency to the organization.
- **Changing impact:** If you are an engineer, your work is no longer merely "managing projects" but ensuring that infrastructure serves and blesses the community.

Realignment consists in injecting your deep desire (the D of DAP.) and your love (the A - *Amour*) into the structure of your current work, transforming it from within. You recover meaning, balance, and fruitfulness—without the stress of an immediate, total change.

Examples:

- **Sarah, an engineer,** realizes that what truly fuels her is not only technical excellence but the way the projects she manages help people live better. She understands that her desire is human impact through technology. She reorients her role toward managing social-impact projects within her company.
- **David, a pastor,** discovers that he finds greater joy in training and inspiring young leaders than in preaching every week. His true

desire is not the stage but transmission and elevation. He develops an intensive mentoring program for future ministries, becoming a trainer rather than a full-time preacher.

In both cases, Sarah and David did not reject their paths; they simply reframed their mission through the lens of their DAP Vision. By listening to their inner fire, they recovered meaning, balance, and fruitfulness.

Thus, the first step in formulating your DAP Vision is to listen to this inner fire—not to restrain it but to consecrate it. It is this fire – guided by faith – that will give you the momentum needed to write your vision—and to live it.

2.4.2. Love: The Condition for Abundance and the Principle of Contribution

If desire is the fire that drives you, love is its spiritual temperature—the divine filter that purifies the flame. Without love, even the noblest desire eventually deteriorates. It turns into empty ambition, a search for recognition, or mere vanity.

Love is not an emotion; it is a spiritual law. Because "God is love" (1 John 4:8), He cannot endorse or sustain a vision that does not reflect His nature. The abundance God grants is never an automatic reward; it is the provision required to accomplish a work rooted in His will and His goodness.

Remember this: when Scripture declares, *"Delight yourself in the Lord, and He will give you the desires of your heart"* (Psalm 37:4), the first part is a condition. To delight in the Lord is to align your project with what delights the heart of God. It is to inscribe your personal vision within His strategy of love, justice, and transformation for the world.

Within the DAP framework, Love becomes the validity condition of your desire. It authorizes only those projects capable of bringing light, elevation, justice, or healing. Love is the criterion through which your vision receives divine approval.

Love: The Living Principle of Contribution

Love prevents desire from turning inward toward ego. It transforms what could have remained a personal ambition into a mission of service. Love elevates your vision:

- from ambition to mission,
- from personal success to collective blessing,
- from the pursuit of results to lasting impact.

Love is the higher law of the Kingdom. It converts every form of success into contribution. And because your project is designed to bless others, you yourself become someone who will be abundantly blessed in return.

Abundance always follows the same path: God entrusts more to those who have proven they know how to redistribute.

Love as the Scale of the Heart

Love continually brings you back to one essential question: *Why are you doing what you are doing?*

It is the spiritual scale that keeps you from building in order to prove something, impress others, or compensate for an inner void. Love frees you from the slavery of human approval. It teaches you to build:

- not to appear successful, but to serve;
- not to elevate yourself, but to elevate others.

When your work flows from your love for God, it becomes a form of worship. When your decisions are guided by love for others, your success becomes a blessing.

Love as a Principle of Impact and Legacy

A vision is truly aligned with love when it contains two essential elements:

1. **Impact** — it genuinely improves the lives of others.
2. **Legacy** — it leaves behind something that continues to bless even in your absence.

Love builds bridges, not walls. It creates solutions that benefit not only you but the entire ecosystem around you—employees, clients, partners, families, and the wider community.

This is the difference between charity, which relieves a moment, and love, which seeks lasting and structural justice.

How to Concretely Integrate Love into Your Vision

Love is the ultimate test of your project's validity. A vision is truly aligned with love when it intentionally integrates both impact and legacy.

Ask yourself the questions of love:

- **Impact:** How will my work or project positively change the lives of others?
- **Quality:** Is my product or service designed with excellence that honors God and respects those it serves?
- **Generosity:** What portion of my success or prosperity do I intentionally allocate to concretely bless a cause, the work of God, or someone in need?

Applying Love to Your Calling

- **If you are an entrepreneur or investor:** Design your project as a solution to a real human need. Place love at the heart of your strategy by valuing employees as collaborators, and by pursuing profit with meaning, never at the expense of meaning.
- **If you are an artist, creative, or communicator:** Do not create merely to shine but to heal, inspire, and elevate. Love is expressed through respect for your audience—by offering content that nourishes and liberates. You place your talent in the service of light, not noise.
- **If you are an educator, coach, or trainer:** Love is expressed through patience and intention. Your mission is not to display what you know but to awaken what others have not yet discovered within themselves. Love teaches you to see in every learner a potential waiting to be revealed.
- **If you are a leader or manager:** Integrate love into your leadership by celebrating the growth of others without fear that they may surpass you. Love is measured by your ability to help others grow without dominating, to correct without humiliating.

An Example of a Project Aligned with the Law of Love: When Love Becomes a Lever for Prosperity

An entrepreneur in the transportation sector develops a logistics company operating between several cities and countries in the region. His objective is clear: grow his fleet, secure major contracts, and build a profitable company capable of ensuring financial stability for his family and his employees. Profit is fully embraced.

But from the outset, he makes a structuring choice: he refuses a form of success built on soulless accumulation. He decides to place his business under a higher law—to honor God and bless others through love. Concretely, he dedicates 10% of his profits to social initiatives and his faith community: support for an orphanage, assistance to a community clinic, scholarships for underprivileged children, and aid to families in distress.

His generosity goes beyond money. Once a month, two trucks deliver essential goods free of charge to remote areas. He pays his drivers fairly, invests in their training, and prioritizes their safety. In his company, money is a tool; love is the direction.

The results follow naturally. Clients recommend him for his integrity, partners prioritize him for his reliability, employees remain loyal, and local authorities facilitate his operations. His company gains a strong reputation, a trusted network, and lasting credibility.

He then discovers a simple and powerful law: what circulates with a pure heart multiplies.

His business is blessed because it blesses. He does not merely transport goods—he allows love to circulate.

2.4.3. Potential: The Capital Within You

An authentic vision is born through a threefold breath. It begins with the whisper of **Desire**—that inner flame that ignites and quietly says, "This is what you deeply want." It is the desirable horizon, the dream that draws you forward. Then comes the firmer voice of **Love,** which provides meaning and structure: "This is what you must do to serve, build, and honor life." It is the ethical imperative, the backbone of the vision. Finally comes the third dimension—often overlooked but decisive: **Potential**, the quiet breath that declares, "This is what you can actually do."

A vision becomes fruitful only when it integrates all three dimensions. Without potential, a dream remains an angel without wings—it inspires but never lands on earth. With potential, vision acquires a body. Potential is the steady force that transforms "I would like to" and "I should" into a credible, embodied, and actionable "I can."

Potential is not guessed; it is analyzed. It does not fall from the sky; it is discovered. It is the living sum of everything you are able to mobilize today—and expand tomorrow—to give form to your vision. It rests on four foundational pillars: natural talents, acquired skills, life experiences, and resources. Together, they constitute your inner capital.

Natural Talents: Innate Capital

Natural talents are the oldest resources within you. They are not learned; they are already there. They are pre-installed inner functions—spontaneous dispositions that allow you to act with ease and accuracy. Where others struggle, you flow. Where others exhaust themselves, you come alive.

A natural talent reveals itself through the convergence of three signs—what we might call a flow of excellence.

First, apparent ease. You accomplish certain tasks without conscious effort, to the point that others are surprised. You are often asked, "How did you do that?" or "Can you explain your method?" What feels ordinary to you is often exceptional to others.

Second, immediate enjoyment, independent of external reward. You lose track of time. You willingly repeat the activity, even without pay, grades, or recognition. This pleasure is a powerful biological and psychological signal: it indicates that you are using a function for which you are naturally wired.

Finally, distinctiveness. What you produce—or the way you produce it—carries your signature. Without trying to be original, you are. Others say, "That's so you."

When ease, pleasure, and distinctiveness overlap, you are looking at a natural talent. It only needs to be acknowledged, tested in real conditions, and then placed in service of an impact that nourishes you rather than consumes you. This is how a gift becomes a sustainable flow of excellence.

Skills: Built Capital

If talents are seeds, skills are muscles. They are not innate; they are built through training, experience, repetition, and discipline. Skills give your potential precision and reliability.

Training provides the theoretical foundation. It structures thinking, offers reference points, and prepares the ground. Whether academic, professional, or self-directed, it represents the first shaping of potential. Moses, educated in Pharaoh's court, later used that formation to lead a people and engage with power.

Professional experience is the test of reality. It confronts theory with the unexpected, forges discernment, and develops character. It is through action that one learns to decide under pressure, manage people, and adapt. David did not become king by decree; he learned courage and strategy through hidden service, tending sheep.

Technical mastery brings accuracy. It enables precise execution, optimized tools, and an often invisible but decisive quality of output. Expertise makes action fluid and credible.

Finally, **discipline** transforms effort into excellence. It takes over when motivation fluctuates. Consistency in practice is what separates the amateur from the professional, passing inspiration from lasting work.

The skills you have already acquired help orient your vision, but they must never limit it. Your potential is evolutionary. You can learn, refine, and expand. Every skill developed is an act of respect toward your potential—and toward those you serve.

Life Experiences: Living Memory

Your life experiences form an inner library. They are not taught in textbooks; they are inscribed in your body, mind, and heart. Every challenge overcome, every responsibility assumed, every wound endured adds a page to this living memory.

Trials forge resilience. Layoffs, failure, loss, and crisis develop an inner strength that no artificial process can produce. Responsibilities mature the soul: carrying a family, a team, or a community expands your capacity to stand under pressure.

Scars, far from being weaknesses, become sources of wisdom. Those who have fallen and risen possess a clarity innocence does not. Some wounds even become missions, when pain is transformed into commitment.

Environment also acts as a silent sculptor. Family, social, cultural, and geopolitical contexts shape values, creativity, and worldview. A human-rights advocate I met in Myanmar—marked by exile and loss—transformed her story into a lifelong commitment to refugees. Her scars became her moral strength.

Your experiences do not define you by what you endured but by what you made of them. They nourish your potential and invite you to transform your story into a legacy.

Resources: The Gold You Can Unlock

Finally come resources—the energy available to move into action. They fall into two categories: human and material.

Human capital is your network: mentors, partners, collaborators, friends, communities. A strong network multiplies capacity, opens doors, and accelerates learning. Many projects succeed not through excess means but through relational quality.

Material capital includes finances, tools, infrastructure, and concrete opportunities. Even modest resources can become powerful when well managed and aligned.

Your environment itself can become a resource: institutions, digital platforms, local knowledge, and cultural wealth. An African farmer, for example, can build a sustainable enterprise by combining ancestral wisdom with modern techniques.

Your resources are the gold you can activate and put to work. They are not only what you possess but what you can activate and transform to move forward. By combining your human capital and material capital, you create a powerful lever—one that gives body to your vision and enables you to move step by step toward your goals.

Potential: What Is Within You to Be Multiplied

Potential is never accidental. It is a sacred deposit—an inner capital placed within every human being with the expectation that it will be developed, cultivated, and multiplied. The parable of the talents reminds us of this truth with great clarity: each person receives something—one talent, two, or five—and God does not ask you to compare what you received with others but to multiply what **you yourself** have received.

The one who buried his talent was not condemned for receiving little but for failing to mobilize his potential.

Your potential is precisely this: what God has entrusted to you so that you may develop it, refine it, and put it to work in service of the Kingdom, the world, and your own destiny.

Potential does not reveal itself in an instant. It unfolds through process—through hidden seasons, quiet training, repeated disciplines, and the small responsibilities you faithfully carry today.

David was not crowned king on the day he was chosen. He learned courage, strategy, and leadership while tending sheep—far from the spotlight, in humble and unseen service. It was there, in the solitude of the pasture, that he forged the skill that later enabled him to face Goliath. This was not a sudden miracle; it was the unveiling of a potential shaped in secrecy.

Moses, too, did not receive his calling without preparation. His education in Pharaoh's court—linguistic, diplomatic, and administrative skills—became the providential tool that enabled him to lead an entire people, stand before kings, and interpret God's will for a nation. What he may have considered a forgotten chapter of his past was in fact a divine investment designed to support his future mission.

So it is with you: nothing in your life is wasted. Your potential is composed of natural gifts, acquired skills, scars transformed into wisdom, and resources you can mobilize—often before you even realize it.

It is by bringing these four dimensions together that you discover what you can truly do—not in imagination but in reality.

And this is where your DAP Vision becomes complete:

- **Desire** reveals what your heart longs to build.
- **Love** reveals what you are called to offer to the world.
- **Potential** reveals the resources you have already been given to begin.

Vision is not wishful projection; it is the meeting point between your inner fire, your sense of responsibility, and your personal capital—much like a craftsman who begins his work using the tools already in his hands.

But the power of the DAP does not lie in the sum of these elements; it is released through their integration. It is when these three forces enter into synergy that what I call a consecrated vision is born—a clear, fruitful, and sustainable vision, capable of attracting divine favor and multiplication.

2.4.4. Practical Exercise: Clarify Your Vision with the DAP (Desire – Love – Potential)

This exercise is designed to help you clearly define your vision.

Step 1: Projection: Visualize Your Ideal Life

Consciously project yourself into the future and visualize your ideal life.

Take time to reflect on the following question, then write freely, without censoring yourself:

What professional and/or economic activities do you see yourself pursuing with joy, passion, and enthusiasm—so much so that you

lose track of time—activities that naturally occupy most of your days and in which you also see yourself prospering?

Write down everything that comes to mind, even if several directions or socio-economic fields emerge. At this stage, you are not choosing—you are observing.

For example:

- professions or vocations,
- entrepreneurial projects,
- business ideas,
- types of investments.

Allow the vision to unfold freely.

Step 2: Impact — Connect Your Vision to Love

Re-read what you have written, then ask yourself this essential question:

By pursuing these socio-economic activities, how do I positively impact humanity, and how can God be glorified through what I do?

Write your answers simply and honestly:

- Who is helped, supported, or transformed by what I create?
- How does this make people's lives more just, dignified, or humane?
- What human, social, or spiritual value is being transmitted?
- How can my income become a channel to bless others and glorify God?

A vision that blesses others and honors God takes deeper root and endures through seasons.

Step 3: Potential —Anchor the Vision in Reality

Now ask yourself this question:

"Do I have the potential to carry out what I have just visualized?"

To answer, observe yourself without judgment:

- what you already know how to do,
- what you have already lived and learned,
- what you currently have at your disposal: time, skills, relationships, material resources.

If the answer is "not yet fully," do not be discouraged. What you are identifying here reflects your current capacity, not your true potential—which is far greater than you may imagine. Potential is never fixed; it grows, expands, and strengthens over time.

Your true treasure also lies in your willingness to learn, to grow, and to discipline yourself. Even if financial or material resources are lacking today, you can rely on your determination, on a clear strategy to build capital, and on your faith in God—the God who declares:

"The silver is mine, and the gold is mine," says the Lord of hosts. — Haggai 2:8

If your network is not yet established, begin by building your capital of credibility: consistency, integrity, and excellence often open doors even before relationships do. Trust the connections that God's grace will bring at the appointed time.

Finally, remember this:

- Your potential is not a limitation, but fertile ground.
- Everything that is missing can be built.

- Everything that is dormant can be awakened.
- Everything that is weak can be strengthened.

Step 4: Formulate Your Vision

Based on everything you have written, now formulate your vision in one or a few clear and simple sentences, combining your desire (dream) and your love (impact).

Read the examples below for inspiration:

- *I am building a leading technology and innovation ecosystem that leverages artificial intelligence and advanced technologies to address major challenges in healthcare. The value created fuels research, local talent development, and innovative entrepreneurship, and a significant portion of this prosperity is dedicated to the work of God, so that technological progress becomes an instrument of life, justice, and hope for millions of people.*
- *I am creating international collections of meaningful luxury clothing and accessories, combining aesthetic excellence with sustainable impact. This project generates shared prosperity: it ensures fair and dignified compensation for artisans and enables me to dedicate 10% of my income to the work of God and charitable causes, so that this abundance becomes a source of Love and transformation.*
- *I invest in the construction and renovation of affordable housing for the middle class, as well as high-end residences. These projects sustainably improve families' quality of life by providing dignified housing adapted to their budgets. They are both a blessing to the households who live there and a lever of abundance for me, enabling me to fund the training of young artisans in sustainable construction techniques and to dedicate 10% of my income to the work of God.*

- *I am building a career of excellence in leadership and sports program management. At the same time, I strategically invest in responsible, value-creating projects to establish stable prosperity. This synergy allows me to have real impact, support educational and social causes, and faithfully dedicate a portion of my income to the work of God, making my professional journey a channel of Love and blessing.*
- *I am building a reference real estate platform dedicated to the development of dignified, accessible, and sustainable housing for the middle class, while also creating high-end residences. Through these projects, I contribute to the lasting transformation of cities, improve the quality of life of thousands of families, and structure a responsible local construction sector. The prosperity generated allows me to invest heavily in training young artisans in sustainable building techniques and to faithfully dedicate 10% of my income to the work of God, so that this growth becomes an instrument of justice, dignity, and large-scale blessing.*

Step 5: Prayer of Vision Consecration

Now pray this prayer to entrust your vision to God.

Heavenly Father,

I consecrate my vision to You.

Align it with Your heart,
and make it an instrument to glorify You and serve others.

Surprise me with Your favor, Your generosity, and Your providence.

Open the doors that no one can shut,
and close those that do not come from You.

I thank You for making me a channel of Your abundance.

May prosperity never imprisons me,
but instead set me free to love, give, and build according to Your will.

In the mighty name of Jesus Christ,
I establish, consecrate, and seal this vision.

Amen.

CHAPTER 3

LONG-TERM GOALS (LTGs): SETTING THE SUMMIT BEFORE CLIMBING THE MOUNTAIN

Introduction: From the Distant Summit to the First Steps

You have already caught a glimpse of your vision in the previous chapter. It stands before you like a majestic mountain—visible, inspiring, calling you forward. It gives direction. It gives meaning. But look closely: no mountain is climbed in a single leap. Every ascent happens step by step, stone by stone, breath after breath.

This is why vision must be translated into goals.

Goals are the steps you place beneath your feet to climb the mountain. They transform the dream into stages. Every great work is built through a succession of small, intentional actions.

That is exactly what this chapter is about: learning how to take your vision—this inspiring picture engraved in your heart—and translate it into concrete, measurable, time-bound goals. Get ready to move from the distant summit you contemplate to the practical steps that carry you forward.

Why Turn Vision into Goals?

A clear vision is like a star in the night sky. It lights up your horizon, draws your gaze forward, and fuels your hope. That star reminds you where you are headed, even when the road feels uncertain. Keeping your eyes fixed on it matters.

But if you only look at the star without ever placing one foot in front of the other, you risk standing still—admiring the destination without ever moving toward it.

Vision is essential because it gives direction. But for vision to become reality, it must be translated into concrete goals. Goals are what create movement. They turn inspiration into action. Vision is born and grows in the heart, but goals bring it down into your hands and your steps.

Goals translate the language of dreams into the language of reality. Without them, vision remains a beautiful idea suspended in the sky. With them, it becomes a work you build day after day.

Biblical Illustration: The Manna in the Wilderness

When Israel left Egypt, God gave them a powerful promise: the Promised Land, flowing with milk and honey. Yet He did not take them there in a single moment. Each day, He gave them a simple, concrete objective: gather enough manna for the day (Exodus 16).

This daily rhythm—ordinary and repetitive—was preparing them for abundance. Their vision was the Promised Land. Their daily goals were to walk, to gather, and to trust.

Let this truth anchor you:

- **Vision gives direction.**
- **Goals give traction.**

Without vision, you wander. Without goals, you stagnate.

But when an inspiring vision is combined with concrete goals, you enter the movement toward the Promised Land—where the dream becomes a path, and the path becomes victory.

3.1. The AMT Method

Your vision is like a seed—full of potential, but destined to remain dormant unless it is planted, watered, and cultivated. The AMT method is that cultivation process. It helps you turn an inspired idea into a structured path.

Your vision is the mountain. Your long-term goals define the specific summit you intend to reach.

If vision shows you the direction, long-term goals give you a clear, measurable, time-bound destination. They are the first step in bringing your vision down from the invisible realm into the visible one.

Long-term goals are the concrete translation of your vision across time. They express what you intend to accomplish over the next three, five, seven, or ten years—whether in your career, your business, or your investments. They function as a stable compass: regardless of storms or detours, you know where you are going.

To formulate them effectively, I invite you to use a simple and powerful framework: the **AMT Method — Ambitious, Measurable, Time-bound.**

This method allows you to articulate your dream into clear, actionable objectives.

3.1.1. A — Ambitious: Dare to Aim High

Your long-term goals should never be limited to simply "being a little better" or "doing a little more." They must represent a horizon that calls you forward—a summit high enough to pull you out of your comfort zone. Ambitious goals stretch you beyond what feels safe and familiar. They compel you to depend on God and to mobilize the very best of your potential.

This is not reckless dreaming. It is faith-filled vision.

An ambitious goal elevates you. It transforms you. It reminds you that—by God's grace—you are capable of crossing mountains others consider impossible.

"Enlarge the place of your tent,
stretch your tent curtains wide,
do not hold back."
— Isaiah 54:2

This verse is more than a metaphor; it is a call to expand your limits.

A truly ambitious goal is not designed to flatter your ego. It forces you to grow—to learn more, to pray more deeply, to surround yourself more wisely, and to plan more intentionally.

Biblical Examples of Inspired Ambition

- **Abraham** had no descendants when God spoke to him about nations. His goal exceeded anything he could produce by human effort alone.

- **Nehemiah** set out to rebuild a ruined wall—in just fifty-two days. An impossible mission, except for a man carried by divine vision.

Your long-term goals should awaken the same blend of awe and conviction within you. If you can accomplish everything without God's help, your goal is too small. But if it leads you to say, "Lord, without You this is impossible—but with You, all things are possible," then you are exactly where you need to be.

An Ambitious Goal...

- Pushes you out of routine and comfort every morning
- Connects you to your full potential and challenges you to rise higher
- Activates your faith, because you rely not only on your resources but on divine provision
- Inspires others, as your growth becomes a living testimony

Why Ambition Is Necessary

- **Because you are moving from Point A to Point B.** You were not created for mediocrity. If your goal remains comfortable and unchallenging, your full potential will never be activated.
- **Because average visions attract little momentum.** Small goals mobilize little energy, little faith, and few resources. Ambitious goals elevate you—and attract the right people, opportunities, and provision.
- **Because ambition is a declaration of faith.** It says, "Lord, I believe You can grow me beyond who I am today. You can train me, equip me, and lift me higher."

How to Formulate an Ambitious Goal

1. **Think big.** Imagine what you would pursue if nothing held you back—no lack of money, no fear, no opinions of others.
2. **Leave your comfort zone.** Choose a goal that invites learning, expansion, and new challenges.
3. **Make room for God.** Healthy ambition does not rely solely on your strength. It says, "With my potential and Your help, Lord, I can," rather than "By myself, I will."
4. **Anchor it in your DAP Vision.**

Remember this: an ambitious goal is not a race against others—it is a calling to become the best version of yourself.

3.1.2. M — Measurable: Establish Clear Benchmarks

An ambitious goal without measurement remains an illusion. You must define clear benchmarks—numbers, results, and concrete indicators—that allow you to know whether you are truly moving forward or simply going in circles. Measurement is the evidence that your vision is leaving the realm of abstraction and entering the realm of construction.

Why Measurement Is Essential

Because without measurement, there is no visible progress. You may carry the most inspiring vision, but if you cannot evaluate what you are accomplishing, you will never know whether you are advancing. Measurement is the language of reality. It transforms intentions into actions, and actions into observable results.

Jesus Himself teaches us the principle of planning and stewardship:

"Suppose one of you wants to build a tower. Won't you first sit down and estimate the cost to see if you have enough money to complete it?" — Luke 14:28

Measuring is not a lack of faith. On the contrary, it is a way of honoring God through responsible stewardship.

Economic Profitability Is Part of Measurement

You have every right to include financial profitability among your goals. In the DAP triangle (Desire – Love – Potential), you may have noticed that I do not speak about chasing money, even though this book addresses prosperity. Why? Because money cannot serve as an inner compass. When a vision is pursued for money alone, it quickly loses meaning, depth, and coherence.

But the opposite extreme is just as dangerous: believing that money is somehow suspect, or incompatible with a life of alignment. In personal and spiritual development, people sometimes avoid speaking honestly about money, as if it were an uncomfortable topic. Yet money is neither impure nor opposed to faith. It is a tool, a legitimate fruit of work, and when managed wisely, it becomes a powerful lever for blessing.

The discomfort around money often comes from confusion: we confuse the obsessive pursuit of money with the legitimate creation of wealth. These two realities are fundamentally different. The first damages the soul. The second strengthens the mission.

Scripture is unambiguous:

"Remember the Lord your God, for it is He who gives you the ability to produce wealth." — Deuteronomy 8:18

This reveals an essential truth: the ability to produce wealth is one of the gifts God gives to humanity. Creating value, generating resources, and building a thriving activity are not spiritual deviations—they are responsibilities.

A project cannot live on inspiration alone. A vision cannot survive on emotion alone. Without a clear economic model, without sustainable income, without value creation, even the most beautiful missions eventually fade away.

Value Creation: The True Measure of Prosperity

That is why economic sustainability should not be seen as a shameful compromise, but as an essential component of a project's strength. It allows the vision to endure, to grow, and to bear fruit over time.

The key, however, is this: it is not about chasing money. It is about focusing on the creation of **VALUE**, with impact in three dimensions:

1. Impact on You — Integral Growth

Abundance begins with you. It enables financial stability, personal growth, and the capacity to support the expansion of your vision. It allows you to live in alignment without compromise.

2. Impact on Others — Multiplication

Your success should never be selfish. A healthy project creates jobs, provides useful services, and offers real solutions. The money you receive is simply the result of the value you bring to others.

3. Impact for God — Testimony

Finally, your abundance should become a tool for greater impact. When it contributes to the advancement of God's Kingdom and the good of others, it becomes a living testimony of God's faithfulness—using the material to serve the spiritual.

Your Challenge

Do not settle for merely earning money. Use your activity to enrich all three dimensions simultaneously. When you commit to creating value for others and for God, material abundance is compelled to follow—because it is needed to sustain the mission entrusted to you.

How to Make Your Goal Measurable

Define clear numbers or specific indicators.

- How many people do you want to reach, train, help, employ, or impact?
- What level of revenue, profitability, or production are you aiming for?

Examples:

- "Train 500,000 young people in digital entrepreneurship."
- "Generate a monthly income of $50,000."

When defining financial metrics—such as revenue, profitability, or income generated by your economic activities—it is essential to intentionally set aside a portion for the work of God and for generosity (tithes, offerings, and charitable giving).

As explained in Chapter 1, this act must not be performed mechanically but with a grateful and joyful heart. It is a conscious acknowledgment that God is the Source of all your resources. Everything you give with love—whether to bless others or to glorify God—returns to you amplified or multiplied.

Examples of Goal Statements Integrating Generosity

1. **Net income objective**
   "Achieve an annual net income of €300,000, including a dedicated allocation of €30,000 for tithes and charitable works."
2. **Margin growth objective**
   "Increase the company's gross margin by 15% by the end of the quarter, ensuring that 10% of this incremental growth is allocated to community projects and the work of God."

Remember this: *"Bring the whole tithe into the storehouse, that there may be food in my house. Test me in this," says the Lord of hosts, "and see if I will not throw open the floodgates of heaven for you and pour out so much blessing that there will not be room enough to store it."* — Malachi 3:10

This is the only verse in the entire Bible where God expressly asks humanity to put Him to the test. God challenges you: test Him and you will see how He will multiply what you give. When you give what you have, God gives what He has, and His reserve is infinite.

Keep this in mind: Measuring is not about limiting oneself. It is giving structure to faith. It is recognizing that God acts through a plan, steps, and results. Your faith produces fruit; measurement allows you to count and celebrate them.

3.1.3. T — Time-Bound: Set a Clear Deadline

An objective without a deadline remains a wish.

It is not yet a commitment, but a beautiful intention suspended in time.

Setting a date is the moment your dream stops being an idea and becomes a project in motion.

"There is a time for everything, and a season for every activity under the heavens." — Ecclesiastes 3:1

God Himself operates within time. He does nothing in haste, yet He leaves nothing undefined. Every divine promise carries not only a purpose but also a season of fulfillment.

When God announced to Abraham that he would have a son, He did not speak in vague terms. He gave a timeline:

"Is anything too hard for the Lord? At the appointed time I will return to you, about this time next year, and Sarah shall have a son." — Genesis 18:14

The promise had a calendar. The promise and the timing were part of the same plan.

Why the Time Factor Is Essential

1. **Time creates accountability** - A deadline forces you to move from reflection to action. It compels you to plan, prioritize, and take concrete steps.
2. **Time protects you from procrastination** - Without a date, there is always a reason to wait for "the right moment." A timeline disrupts indecision and inertia.

3. **Time structures your faith** - Setting a deadline is saying to God: "Here is my faith in action. I believe You can help me accomplish this within this season."

The calendar becomes a spiritual tool—an expression of trust in divine timing.

A Contemporary Example: Fred Swaniker

Fred Swaniker, founder of African Leadership University (Ghana), did not simply say, "I want to train African leaders."

He set a clear target: to train 25,000 young African leaders by 2035.

That temporal clarity mobilized investors, faculty, partners, and students across the continent. Time became a driver of vision.

Swaniker's story powerfully illustrates that faith and calendars work together.

- His intention was deep—having experienced leadership instability in Africa from the age of four.
- His potential was ready—McKinsey, Stanford, Arjay Miller Scholar.
- But what transformed an idea (a business plan written at Stanford) into African Leadership University—described by CNN as "the Harvard of Africa"—was the courage to date the vision.

By publicly committing to training 25,000 leaders by 2035—and later 3 million leaders by 2060—Swaniker did three things aligned with the AMT framework:

1. **He eliminated vagueness** - A vague goal is a missed target waiting to happen. Clear dates forced rigorous planning, infrastructure

development, and the opening of campuses in Mauritius and Kigali.

2. **He attracted major allies** - A measurable and time-bound vision convinced Silicon Valley investors that this was not a noble idea but a serious strategy. Leaders such as Graça Machel (Chancellor) and Donald Kaberuka (Board Member) joined the project. Precise timelines attract serious resources.
3. **He created positive urgency** - Deadlines ignite action. Like Abraham walking toward the Promised Land before possessing it, Swaniker launched his academy immediately after graduating in 2004. Time forced movement.

Time, therefore, is not a constraint. It is the structural frame that gives your vision enough weight to materialize.

By dating your Long-Term Goals (LTGs), you declare not only your faith in fulfillment but also your readiness to steward the rhythm of the abundance that is coming.

Abraham and Swaniker remind us of the same truth: **A vision becomes powerful when it is anchored in a calendar.**

How to Give Your Objective a Time Dimension (T)

The time dimension is what transforms vague hope into an action plan. To anchor your vision in a real timeline for fulfillment, here are two fundamental principles to follow:

1. Set a Clear Completion Date — The Act of Prophetic Commitment

Define precisely when you commit to achieving your objective. This commitment should be as specific as a business contract or a biblical promise.

Examples:

- "By **December 2028**, I will publish three books reaching 500,000 readers."
- "**Within three years**, I will generate a sustainable monthly income of USD 25,000 through my digital services company."

A date is a concrete prophecy.

It creates expectation and preparation, forcing your mind to search for solutions before the deadline arrives.

When you assign a number and a month to your dream, you make it tangible. You create creative tension—the gap between your present reality and your defined future. That tension is one of the most powerful engines of action.

2. Be Firm on Direction, Flexible on Timing: The Wisdom of Habakkuk

Life is not linear.

The road to abundance often includes straight paths, detours, and seasons of waiting.

- **Do not confuse delay with defeat.**

A delay is not failure if direction remains intact. It may be a season of maturation—where God is equipping you, aligning resources, or preparing encounters beyond your control.

- **Anchor yourself in Scripture:**

"For the vision is yet for an appointed time... Though it delays, wait for it; it will surely come, it will not delay." — Habakkuk 2:3

A deadline is a guide, not an idol.

If you remain faithful in the process—advancing with discipline and faith—time becomes your ally, not your judge.

Faith asks you to set the date. Wisdom asks you to honor the process.

3.2. An Ambitious, Measurable, and Time-Bound Objective Becomes an Embodied Promise— A project you can visualize, plan, track, and celebrate.

Below are a few examples of long-term AMT objectives.

Example 1: Green Energy Consulting

By March 2029 (T), establish my green energy consulting firm and position it as a leading reference in the regional market (A). This commitment will translate into the achievement of €5 million in annual revenue (M), ensuring full financial freedom (A), while guaranteeing—starting from the first profitable year—the measurable and prioritized allocation of 10% of net profit (M) to charitable works and to the glory of God.

AMT Breakdown

CRITERION	OBJECTIVE DETAIL	WHY IT IS STRONGER
A – Ambitious	Market leadership; financial freedom; prioritized 10% allocation for the glory of God	The ambition is high (regional leadership) and purified by the consecration of part of the results to service. This elevates the objective from a goal to a mission.
M – Measurable	50 employees; €5 million in annual revenue; 10% of net profit allocated	Generosity (10% of net profit) is quantified and integrated as a performance indicator, proving that giving is an essential component of profitability.
T – Time-Bound	March 2029	A precise deadline creates positive urgency and clear commitment.

Example 2: Spiritual Publishing & Mission

By the end of 2030 (T), publish a trilogy of spiritual books (A) reaching a cumulative audience of 1.5 million readers (M). This body of work will generate USD 180,000 in net annual passive income (M), enabling us to fully fund a dedicated missionary project without relying on external donations.

AMT Justification

Criterion	**Explanation**
A – Ambitious	Reaching 1.5 million readers with a trilogy requires high faith, strategic marketing, and exceptional quality. Fully funding a missionary project through passive income is the ultimate expression of service-oriented intention and faith in multiplication.
M – Measurable	1.5 million cumulative readers and USD 180,000 in net annual passive income. These figures measure both impact and profitability and are intentionally calibrated to fully cover the operational costs of the missionary project, ensuring sustainability and independence.
T – Time-Bound	End of 2030 (allowing sufficient time to write, publish, and build a lasting audience across multiple books).

3.3. Practical Exercise: Formulate Your LTGs Using the AMT Method

This exercise marks a turning point.

You are no longer just imagining your ideal life—you are writing it into time, making it measurable and concrete.

Remember: Your vision is the mountain, but your long-term objectives define the summit.

So take a quiet moment, notebook in hand, and allow God to inspire you as you write.

Step 1: Reconnect With Your DAP Vision

Review the vision you defined in the previous chapter (integrating your Desire, Love, and Potential).

Ask yourself:

"What major achievements would I like to see accomplished in the next 3, 5, or 7 years if I were to put all my strength—and my faith—at the service of my vision?"

Write freely, without censoring yourself.

Your objective must be "A" – Ambitious

Dare to dream big. Your objective should be larger than you, require dependence on God, and push you to grow.

Ask yourself:

- **If I had no fear, no limitations, and no financial constraints, what would I undertake?**
- **Does my objective reflect my calling—not just my comfort?**

Your objective must be "M" – Measurable

An ambitious objective must be measurable. Define concrete benchmarks: numbers, visible outcomes, and indicators of progress.

Ask yourself:

- **How will I know that my objective has been achieved?**
- **What numbers, tangible results, or transformations will prove it?**

- **Does my objective include an economic profitability dimension?**
- **What amount or percentage will be dedicated to God's work and to generosity?**

Your objective must be "T" – Time-Bound

An objective without a deadline remains a good intention. Assign it a precise date—this creates discipline, motivation, and faith oriented toward fulfillment.

Ask yourself:

- **How long do I want to take to reach this summit?**
- **What is a realistic yet challenging date that pushes me to act today?**
- **What could I accomplish each year to move closer to it?**

Step 2: Combine the AMT Elements

Now assemble all the elements into clear, inspiring, and powerful sentences.

These become your **AMT long-term goals**—the visible fruit of your DAP vision.

CHAPTER 4

SHORT-TERM GOALS (STGs): THE RHYTHM OF PROGRESS

Introduction: Daily Small Wins

The mountain of vision is never climbed in a single day. After boldly defining your long-term summit (Long-Term Goals – LTGs), the time has come to stop merely contemplating the peak and start preparing the climb. It is in this critical transition that Short-Term Goals (STGs) are born—those regular, measurable victories that transform an intimidating dream into steady, controlled progress.

STGs are the daily, operational seeds of your vision. They represent what you want and are able to accomplish concretely over the next 3, 6, or 12 months. If your LTGs define the strategic destination, your STGs form the clearly marked path—step by step—ensuring that you are in constant motion and heading in the right direction.

Why Short-Term Goals Are the Keystone

A dream only gains substance when it begins to take shape in the present. STGs are that practical embodiment. They are not a simple to-do list;

they are an essential psychological and spiritual mechanism that gives substance, rhythm, and unshakable discipline to your greater vision.

- **They build discipline** - You learn to build not in the euphoria of sudden motivation but through measured consistency. Discipline is choosing action when feelings are absent.
- **They nourish practical faith** - Each small success, each box checked, becomes tangible proof that progress is possible—and that God is active even in details and small beginnings. The invisible becomes visible.
- **They sustain motivation** - A sense of accomplishment, however small, creates a positive feedback loop. Visible progress renews courage and energy, especially during seasons of discouragement or waiting.
- **They structure meaning** - STGs answer the question: "Why did I get up this morning?" You know exactly why you are working and how each hour and effort contributes to reaching your summit.

STGs are like the stones of a mountain trail: modest, often repetitive—but without them, the ascent becomes slippery, and the summit remains unreachable.

4.1. How to Define Clear, Operational "SMART" STGs

After determining the altitude of your LTGs, it is time to define the concrete steps that will take you there. An effective STG must be a clear and powerful action:

- **Specific** (you know exactly what needs to be done),
- **Measurable** (you can verify whether it has been completed),

- **Achievable** within a short timeframe (3, 6, or 12 months),
- **Directly connected** to your vision and your LTGs.

The Key Question

"What critical and meaningful step can I accomplish within the next 3, 6, or 12 months that will undeniably move me closer to my vision and long-term objectives?"

Examples of STGs

To grasp the power of this breakdown, consider these clear transitions from a distant dream to a first meaningful step:

- If your LTG is to **build a house**, your STG is to **purchase the land**.
- If your LTG is to **become an author**, your STG is to **write and revise the first five chapters of your manuscript**.
- If your LTG is to **change careers and become a software developer within three years**, your initial STG is to **complete an introductory coding course (e.g., Python or JavaScript) and build two small practical projects within 90 days**.
- If your LTG is to **launch an online artisanal products business**, your essential STG is to **create the online store (platform selection and design) and produce an initial inventory of 50 items ready to ship within four months**.
- If your LTG is to **master a new language (e.g., Spanish) for travel**, your measurable STG is to **learn 500 core vocabulary words and hold a five-minute basic conversation on everyday topics within six months**.

4.2. STGs: The Law of Small Seeds and the Power of Compound Growth

Your STG is not "too small." It is the essential beginning. It aligns with the biblical wisdom of compounded growth through small acts:

- A small jar of flour was multiplied to feed an entire family (1 Kings 17:8–16).
- A mustard seed, the smallest of all seeds, becomes a great tree where the birds of the air find shelter (Luke 13:18–19).

Your short-term objective is that humble seed—carrying within it the full potential of a great tree.

The Most Dangerous Trap: Despising the Humility of First Steps

Many people abandon their vision not because it is too big but because they despise the humility and ordinariness of the first steps. We want the extraordinary without embracing the ordinary.

Yet it is patient accumulation that creates unstoppable momentum:

- Reading 10 pages a day (over 3,600 pages a year).
- Writing 30 minutes every morning (enough to produce a full first draft of a book within a few months).
- Making 3 client calls a day (generating 750 interactions per year).

These small actions create a powerful compound effect. This is the **Law of Consistency and Daily Faithfulness**: what you do in small measure, but regularly and faithfully, becomes a force capable of moving mountains. Consistency beats intensity.

Examples of Short-Term Goals (STGs)

Below are concrete examples of STGs across different sectors, illustrating how vision becomes action through humble, disciplined steps:

Film / Production. Write and revise the complete screenplay for a short film (or a TV series pilot) focused on reconciliation, and secure a minimum production budget commitment of €5,000 within 4 months.

Logistics / Transportation. Complete a fleet management training program and obtain all required licenses and insurance for freight transportation within 4 months.

Engineering / Real Estate. Define and automate a savings strategy to set aside 10% of salaried income for real estate investment, and study three potential neighborhoods for a first acquisition within 12 months.

AI / Healthcare. Develop a prototype early-detection algorithm for a specific rare disease and achieve an initial 75% accuracy rate on a selected test dataset within 6 months.

Ethical Fashion / Luxury. Produce an initial capsule collection of 10 pieces with local artisans, while documenting real production costs and fair compensation within 5 months.

Hospitality / Gastronomy. Finalize the detailed menu for the first restaurant, establish formal partnerships with three high-quality local suppliers, and complete the financial feasibility study within 3 months.

Beauty / Wellness. Launch a pilot online store with an initial range of five premium cosmetic products and achieve 50 first sales within 90 days.

Interior Design / Coaching. Launch a 4-week online mentorship program focused on women's financial empowerment and enroll 20 paying participants within 3 months.

Logistics / Transportation (Personal Growth Path). Rigorously save 75% of net income from current taxi-driving activity to accumulate €3,500 in startup capital for the acquisition of a first vehicle within 12 months.

Real Estate / Construction. Identify, negotiate, and secure an option on a viable first plot of land for an affordable or luxury housing project within 8 months, while establishing a quantified financing plan (bank financing and/or savings).

Personal Finance / General. Establish systematic tithing (10% of income) and a regular charitable contribution to an organization serving underprivileged children, and maintain this discipline consistently for 12 months.

4.3. A Balance to Preserve: Short-Term Objectives across All Dimensions of Life

Even though the initial momentum of your Long-Term Goals (LTGs) is primarily focused on your career, business, or investment ambitions (and this is indeed the central focus of this book), it is essential to intentionally integrate Short-Term Goals (STGs) that address other key areas of life—especially your spiritual life, relational and social life, and physical and mental well-being.

Your life is a coherent whole.

Isolated professional success, disconnected from these dimensions, remains fragile and unsustainable. That is why I strongly encourage you to extend your STGs to the other foundational pillars of a balanced and fruitful life.

The Spiritual Dimension: The Invisible Fuel

Sustainable success is always fueled by an inexhaustible inner source. Neglecting the spiritual dimension inevitably leads to burnout—even at the peak of material achievement.

The principle *"Seek first the Kingdom of God, and all these things will be added to you"* (Matthew 6:33) is not symbolic; it is the law of divine priority. When alignment is established, everything else finds its proper place and rhythm.

This dimension is about cultivating intimacy and dependence. It is not enough to believe—you must practice the presence of God. This requires intentionally setting apart time for prayer, silence, and meditation on Scripture. It is in this sacred space that discernment is sharpened and decisions are purified from anxiety and greed.

These invisible disciplines strengthen your soul, clarify your judgment, and anchor you in a deep, unshakable peace—the true foundation of long-term perseverance.

The Relational and Social Dimension: No One Builds Alone

Human beings are not islands. Even the most solitary destiny is shaped through the gaze, support, and sometimes the loving confrontation of others.

Any form of success that isolates you, fractures relationships, or requires stepping on others will eventually turn against you. True success is not measured only by what you achieve or possess but by who you become in relationship—as a partner, parent, friend, mentor, neighbor, and citizen.

Your STGs must therefore include concrete relational objectives: restoring broken trust, nurturing long-standing friendships, showing up during critical moments, learning to listen without judgment, or creating spaces for collective contribution.

In today's hyperconnected world, it is easy to confuse contacts with connections. Yet relational depth is built through small, repeated acts of faithfulness: a message sent after a difficult season, a meal without an agenda, a conflict resolved before nightfall, a boundary respected quietly. These gestures weave the invisible social fabric that will support you when your inner strength falters.

Be mindful of the mirror effect: you often attract who you have become. If ambition makes you critical, suspicious, or calculating, your relationships will reflect hardness. If you cultivate generosity, clarity, and loyalty, you will eventually be surrounded by people who mirror those same qualities.

This is why it is wise to integrate a yearly relational audit into your STGs:

- Who inspires me?
- Who drains me?
- Who sanctifies me?
- Who lovingly challenges me?

Sometimes, wisdom requires disengaging from toxic relationships—not with bitterness but with clarity and resolve. Other times, it requires reinvesting in relationships you have neglected under the excuse of "lack of time."

Social life is not an optional extra—it is an ecosystem. When you isolate yourself to "save time," you impoverish the very soil from which future ideas, partnerships, opportunities, and support will grow. Integrate objectives that keep you rooted: a weekly meal with loved ones, a group where honest conversations happen, or a volunteer commitment that reminds you that you are not the center of the world.

These relational investments do not distract you from your mission; they extend its longevity by keeping you human, grounded, and connected.

The Physical and Mental Well-Being Dimension: The Body as Stewardship

"Your body is the temple of the Holy Spirit" (1 Corinthians 6:19).

Neglecting your health is compromising the very vehicle of your vision. Physical energy sustains spiritual endurance and professional productivity. Strong physical discipline often reflects strong mental discipline.

Health—both physical and mental—is not a luxury; it is responsible stewardship. It involves sleep quality, balanced nutrition, regular physical activity, and the humility to rest when your body demands it.

Exhaustion is not a sign of virtue; it is often a sign of poor management. By honoring your body, you preserve vitality and resilience, enabling you to run the long race, honor your commitments, and receive prosperity without collapsing under its weight.

Examples of Balanced STGs

Spiritual Anchoring. Dedicate 15 minutes each morning to silence and biblical meditation, free from digital distractions. Maintain this discipline for 12 consecutive months.

Family Quality Time. Plan and honor a weekly 3-hour family evening with your spouse and children, with no professional interruptions, for the next 12 weeks.

Physical Vitality. Complete three physical activity sessions per week (30–60 minutes of brisk walking, running, swimming, or gym workouts) and track your progress over the next quarter.

Mental Hygiene. Improve sleep quality by establishing a strict evening routine—no screens 60 minutes before bedtime—to achieve an average of 7.5 hours of sleep per night for six months.

Relational Restoration. Reconnect with five close friends or mentors you have neglected by scheduling a meaningful meal or conversation with each within 90 days.

Intellectual Growth. Complete one selected theological or personal development book and synthesize five key principles applicable to your life within four months.

Deliberate Nutrition. Eliminate sugary drinks and ultra-processed foods entirely for 90 days, maintaining strict adherence throughout the period.

Relational Clarity. Conduct a personal relational audit. Identify two toxic relationships to distance yourself from, and actively seek one inspiring mentor or coach for the next six months.

4.4. Exercise: Define Your Short-Term Goals (STGs)

This exercise transforms your vision and Long-Term Goals (LTGs) into concrete, achievable actions for the coming months. It is intentionally simple because Short-Term Goals must be clear, practical, and immediately actionable.

Step 1: Socio-Economic STGs – The Engine

Revisit your intention, your vision, and your LTGs.

Then ask yourself this single, decisive question:

"What, within the next 3, 6, or 12 months, will prove that I have moved forward toward my DAP Vision and my LTGs—while honoring God with my passions, my love, my talents, and my finances?"

Identify and list your key domains. These are the socio-economic pathways defined in the previous chapters and articulated in your DAP Vision:

- Employment / Career
- Entrepreneurship
- Investments

Examples of socio-economic STG domains:

- **Grow:** skills development and performance in my current role
- **Create:** launch a service, product, or content
- **Structure:** organize my finances, save, and invest

Do not forget to include an STG dedicated to generosity. Set aside a portion of your income for God's work (tithe, offerings, and donations). This act must never be mechanical but intentional and grateful—acknowledging God as the Source of all your resources. What you give with love always returns multiplied.

Example of a Generosity STG:

"Starting this month, faithfully set aside 10% of all net income (tithe and offerings) for God's work and acts of generosity, prayerfully guided by the Holy Spirit, and maintain this discipline through December 31."

Step 2: Add Balance STGs

List some balance-oriented STGs in the following dimensions:

- Spiritual
- Social and relational
- Physical and mental well-being

These objectives protect your long-term sustainability and ensure that your progress remains aligned, healthy, and integrated.

Step 3: Write Your STGs

Using the examples shared throughout this chapter, clearly formulate your own Short-Term Goals.

Each STG should be:

- Specific
- Measurable
- Time-bound
- Directly connected to your vision and LTGs

Step 4: Validate Your STGs with Faith and Discernment

For each STG, ask yourself the following questions—and answer them with unwavering faith:

- **"Can I realistically accomplish this within the defined timeframe using my current resources and/or by relying on God's grace?"**
- **"Does this objective truly move me closer to my intention, my DAP Vision, and my LTGs?"**

If the answer is yes to both questions, you have a solid STG.

If not, simplify it, adjust the scope, or reformulate it until clarity and alignment are restored.

Key Reminder

Short-Term Goals are not about pressure—they are about alignment. They are the faithful steps through which vision becomes obedience, discipline becomes fruitfulness, and faith becomes visible progress.

CHAPTER 5

ATTENTION: CLAIMING YOUR VICTORY BY FAITH

Introduction: Focused and Repeated Attention—the Crucible of Unshakable Faith

Once your vision and objectives are clearly established, they must not be pushed to the margins of your life or abandoned to the forgetfulness of good intentions. They must become the living center of your attention, nourished by unshakable faith and translated into concrete, aligned action. What you desire to manifest cannot survive neglect. Do not let it sleep. Keep it with you. Return to it constantly. Carry it daily.

This is why it is essential to materialize your vision and goals on one or more tangible supports of your choice—a notebook, a board, images, objects—so that you can maintain regular, conscious, and faith-filled contact with them. What is not recalled weakens, and what is not maintained withers.

The intention, vision, and abundance-oriented goals you have established are great and ambitious; they do not yield to a distracted mind. They require voluntary, intense, and fully directed attention. Every time your mind deliberately returns to your aspirations, you are not merely thinking about the future—you are imprinting the promise into your consciousness, engraving it into your heart, and exposing it to the living light of faith, where it takes root, gains strength, and acquires substance.

This repeated return acts like a seed watered with consistency: it nourishes your inner conviction and progressively aligns your thoughts, emotions, and decisions with what you are called to accomplish. Gradually, your entire being comes into harmony with your vision.

Focused attention is neither carnal obsession nor an escape from reality. It is a spiritual discipline—a deliberate and daily renewed choice to decide what is allowed to dwell in your mind. For what you contemplate persistently, what you nourish through your thoughts, emotions, and persevering prayer, inevitably grows, takes root, and manifests in your reality.

But remember this: power does not reside in attention alone. Power resides above all in faith. Focused and repeated attention sustains faith, while faith charges attention with irresistible spiritual and emotional force. Without faith, repeated attention becomes a mechanical exercise. Faith is a deep conviction, an unshakable certainty that what you pursue is already accomplished in the invisible—even if nothing yet confirms it in the visible.

"Now faith is the assurance of things hoped for, the conviction of things not seen."
— Hebrews 11:1

It is this assurance that unlocks the doors of success and gives birth to the miracle you are expecting. Remember the words of Jesus in the Gospels: "Your faith has healed you" and "Your faith has saved you."

Focused and repeated attention remains essential because it feeds faith. By keeping your gaze fixed on your vision, you allow your conviction to take root, to strengthen, and to grow. It becomes an inner power, supported by a discipline of the mind that refuses dispersion and chooses, again and again, to turn toward the image of the promised success.

Regular contact with your embodied dream acts as a constant reminder—a living anchor that sustains focused attention and nourishes faith day after day.

5.1. Materialization: The First Tangible Manifestation of Your Dreams

Materialization is the act through which the invisible begins its journey toward the visible. It is the breaking point with abstraction. As long as your vision and goals remain confined within the corridors of your mind, they are subject to mood fluctuations, waves of doubt, and the erosion of forgetfulness. By projecting them outside yourself onto a physical support, you proclaim that your dream is no longer a mere "idea" but a reality in the process of formation.

When you write your intention and your DAP Vision, when you display your Long-Term Goals (LTGs) and Short-Term Goals (STGs), when you choose images, words, symbols, or objects that represent what you are pursuing, you are doing far more than organizing your thoughts. You are creating a point of contact between your dream and the real world. This materialization is not merely meant to make your dreams visible; it is primarily a way to maintain regular contact with your aspirations and to nurture and sustain unshakable faith. For what fulfills a dream is not its definition but the faith and action that accompany it.

"Write the vision; make it plain on tablets, so he may run who reads it." — Habakkuk 2:2

This is not simply about having a vision but about fixing it on tangible supports so that it becomes visible, readable, accessible, and repeatable. A vision that can be reread, reviewed, and felt regularly is a vision that can be believed. It works on your subconscious, takes root within you, and becomes familiar. What is materialized—written, drawn, displayed, symbolized—no longer depends on fragile memory or momentary emotion. It enters time.

Each repeated contact with this support becomes an act of remembrance, a silent sermon preached to your own heart. You no longer need to convince yourself—the vision speaks to you, day after day.

When you read your vision, when your eyes contemplate it, when your mouth proclaims it, when your hands have written it, you engage your entire being in a single movement. Your vision and objectives cease to be imaginary, intellectual, or abstract; they become embodied. This process gradually transforms your inner world until believing becomes natural.

Prayer, when combined with this regular contact, acts like a divine breath upon what is written. You are not merely looking at a vision—you are continually presenting it to God, reminding Him of it, and aligning yourself with it. What you pray over consistently, with gratitude and faith, acquires a spiritual density that nothing can shake.

By contrast, what remains only thought or imagined stays vague, unstable, and easily replaced by urgencies, fears, or distractions. A vision that is not materialized is like a seed kept in the hand: it holds potential, but it will bear no fruit until it is planted in the ground.

Thus, materialization becomes a concrete act of faith. It declares to the visible world what your heart already believes in the invisible. It affirms that your vision deserves space, time, and attention. And it is precisely this consistency—supported by prayer, nourished by attention, and sealed by faith—that transforms a dream into a manifested reality.

5.1.1. Materialization Tools: Finding Your Anchor Point

There is no single, universal, or "perfect" tool for materializing your vision. There is your tool—the one that creates for you a living, regular, and deep connection with what you are called to manifest.

The previous chapters have helped you clarify your intention, your vision, and your goals. From this point on, the challenge is no longer what to pursue but how to remain consistently and meaningfully connected to that vision. The right tool is the one that gently yet firmly brings you back to your vision—not through constraint but through inner attraction.

This tool may be written, visual, auditory, symbolic, artistic, or even hybrid. It may take the form of a notebook, images, spoken words, objects, diagrams, or personal creations. Its form is secondary. What truly matters is its ability to become a daily anchor for your attention and a source of nourishment for your faith.

A truly effective tool acts as a living reminder. It reconnects you to your vision when doubt arises, recenters your mind when distraction threatens, and rekindles your conviction when emotion fades. Each encounter with it becomes a silent act of faith—a way of telling your heart: what I am pursuing is real, legitimate, and already in motion.

Do not try to imitate an external model. Explore, experiment, and adjust. Allow yourself to be guided by what resonates deeply within you. For power does not reside in the form of the tool but in the inner relationship you cultivate with it. It is this relationship—nourished by attention, sealed by faith, and extended through action—that opens the passage between the invisible and the visible.

Multiple Tools, One Focus

There is not a single legitimate tool for materializing your vision but several gateways toward the same objective: keeping your attention alive and nurturing unshakable faith. Each tool engages a specific dimension of your being—intellect, emotion, speech, body, or imagination. It is up to you to discern the one—or the combination—that resonates most deeply with your personal sensitivity.

The Vision–Goals Notebook: The Foundational Anchor

The Vision–Goals Notebook is a written tool dedicated exclusively to your intention, your vision, and your goals. Its purpose is to gather, in one place, your intention, your overarching vision, and your objectives, giving them a tangible, stable, and accessible existence.

Concretely, it means putting into words—clearly and deliberately—what you are pursuing: the direction you have chosen, the major milestones to be reached, and the concrete steps that will take you there. By writing, you bring your dream down from the invisible into the visible. You move from a floating idea to a written promise—one that can be reread, owned, and claimed.

To write is to fix. Every word inscribed gives lasting form to what your heart already believes. With each rereading, your conviction deepens and your mind realigns. The notebook becomes an external memory that protects your dream from doubt, forgetfulness, and dispersion.

When used consistently, it becomes an anchor of faith. Each written word is a seed. Each rereading is watering. Just as Abraham lifted his eyes toward the stars to remember God's promise, you open your notebook to contemplate your vision. It is no longer merely an organizational tool but a prophetic instrument that nourishes your faith and brings you back, day after day, to what truly matters.

The Vision Board: Vision That Awakens Emotion

The Vision Board is a visual tool for conscious projection. It consists of gathering, on a single physical or digital space, images, words, symbols, and sometimes Scripture verses that concretely represent the life, goals, and inner state you desire to manifest.

In practice, it is not a simple aesthetic collage but an intentional staging of your future. Each image is chosen not for what it objectively depicts but for the emotion it awakens within you and the spiritual meaning it carries. The Vision Board translates your vision into a visual language that is directly accessible to your subconscious.

Where writing structures thought, images make the promise come alive. By regularly exposing your eyes to these representations, you allow your mind to integrate your vision as an already familiar reality. Images speak effortlessly—without argument, without resistance. They become silent prophecies that nourish faith.

Placed within your daily environment, this embodied vision acts like a window opened onto your future. It keeps your attention focused, awakens the right emotion, and gradually aligns your thoughts, decisions, and actions with what you are called to manifest. Just as God showed Abraham the stars to strengthen his faith, your Vision Board becomes a personal sky filled with promises. Every glance is a reminder. Every emotion felt is a seed. And this repetition strengthens your inner certainty.

Vocal Affirmations: The Spoken Word That Seals Faith

Vocal affirmations are an auditory tool of conscious proclamation. They consist of expressing your vision and goals in the form of positive declarations, then speaking them aloud and hearing them regularly. What you are doing here is not wishing—it is proclaiming.

The voice is not neutral. It creates. Scripture reminds us that "faith comes from hearing" (Romans 10:17). When you hear your own voice affirming what you are pursuing, your words become spiritual seeds and an inner programming. They shape your subconscious, align your mind, and prepare your entire being to act in coherence with what you declare.

Practically, this tool is based on auditory repetition. By regularly listening to statements that express your vision as an already-engaged reality, you transform vague hope into rooted conviction. The tone, intonation, and emotion carried by your voice add an affective and spiritual charge that strengthens faith and makes the promise inwardly credible.

Used in daily life, vocal affirmations become a prophetic echo that accompanies you. They recenter your mind in moments of distraction, rekindle faith in seasons of doubt, and keep your attention aligned with your vision. Each listening is a reminder. Each spoken word is a stone laid on the path toward manifestation.

Thus, where the notebook fixes the vision and images awaken it, the voice seals it. Just as Abraham contemplated the stars to remember the promise, you lend your ear to your own words to hear—again and again—the vision God has placed within you, until it becomes obvious, natural, and alive.

Artistic Expression: Vision Embodied Through Creativity

Artistic expression is a creative tool for materialization. It consists of representing your vision and goals through drawings, sketches, diagrams, or illustrated mind maps. Here, you no longer merely write or look—you create. You engage your imagination, your body, and your emotions in a single act.

Art is a language that transcends words. Where writing structures thought and images inspire, drawing allows you to express vision in an intuitive, personal, and emotional way. By transforming your goals into shapes, colors, and symbols, you give your dream a unique visual signature that speaks directly to your subconscious.

Concretely, this tool may take the form of simple sketches, illustrated mind maps, drawn scenes, or abstract symbols. Artistic quality is irrelevant. What matters is not aesthetics but meaning. Even the simplest drawing carries symbolic power when it is charged with intention and faith.

By drawing yourself, you embody the vision through movement. Every line becomes a silent declaration, every color an emotion, every symbol a promise. Artistic expression thus acts as an active visualization: you do not merely see your future—you shape it inwardly.

When used regularly, it stimulates creativity, strengthens memory, and creates an intimate bond with your vision. Just as God gave Abraham concrete images to strengthen his faith—the stars, the sand—you create your own images to nourish your conviction. Your sketch becomes an anticipated proof of what is to come, a living bridge between imagination and faith.

The Digital Sanctuary: Sanctifying Everyday Space

The digital sanctuary is a manifestation tool integrated into your daily environment. It consists of transforming the tools you use most—phone, computer, and tablet— into conscious reminder spaces for your vision. Where your attention is often captured by the outside world, you intentionally inscribe your inner promise.

Practically, this tool takes the form of meaningful wallpapers, symbolic images, key phrases, or affirmations, combined with scheduled reminders that appear at strategic moments throughout the day. Each notification then becomes a sacred interruption—a discreet but regular call back to what truly matters.

The digital sanctuary works through gentle repetition. Without requiring deliberate effort, it redirects your gaze, realigns your mind, and rekindles faith at the very heart of your ordinary activities. What was once a tool of distraction becoming an instrument of recentering and consecration.

By sanctifying your digital space, you refuse to leave your attention to chance. You choose what enters your mind and what shapes your inner world. Each visual or auditory reminder becomes a seed. Each return to the image or the word reinforces the conviction that your vision is alive, active, and already in motion.

Thus, even amid noise, urgency, and screens, you create a space of inner silence—a place where your vision speaks to you, day after day. A discreet yet powerful sanctuary where the invisible continues to take shape in the visible.

The Memory Object and Intentional Artifact: Vision Embodied in Matter

The intentional object or artifact is a tactile tool of materialization. It consists of choosing, carrying, or placing within your immediate environment a physical element that symbolizes a crucial aspect of your vision. Here, vision leaves the realm of concept, image, or sound and acquires weight, texture, and physical presence. It becomes something you can grasp, touch, and feel.

Touch is one of the most ancient and powerful senses for anchoring certainty. Where the notebook structures and the vision board inspire, the object testifies. It serves as a bridge between the invisible world of your aspirations and the concrete reality of your daily life. By holding this object, you send a signal to both your brain and your spirit that your vision is not a mere fiction but a reality in the process of incarnation.

Practically, this support can take many forms: a key on your desk symbolizing the opening of a new door, a bracelet engraved with a keyword, a polished stone representing the solidity of your faith, or even a specific garment that evokes the identity of the person you are becoming. What matters is not the market value of the object but the symbolic charge you have intentionally placed upon it. It becomes a portable memorial.

Placed within your field of action—on your bedside table, in your pocket, or on your workspace—the object acts as a physical sentinel. Each time your hand brushes against it or your eyes rest upon it, it triggers an immediate reminder. It bypasses complex reasoning and brings your attention back to the essential in a fraction of a second. It is an anchor that prevents drift when the winds of doubt or fatigue arise.

Used with intention, the object becomes an instrument of remembrance. Just as Joshua instructed the people to set up stones after crossing the

Jordan so that every glance would tell the story of God's faithfulness, your memory object becomes a silent witness to your journey. It reminds you that, just as this object exists here and now in your hands, your vision already possesses substance. Every physical contact becomes an act of reaffirmation—a way of saying: "What I hope for is as real as what I touch."

It is essential to understand that these objects have no magical or esoteric power. They are not talismans. A key placed on a desk does not possess any mystical ability to open doors; it is simply a reminder and a psychological tool meant to focus and hold your attention. The power lies in your relationship with God and in your actions, not in the object itself.

5.1.2. The Alchemy of Supports: Freedom in Service of Faith

This list of supports is not a closed system but an open doorway into the full range of your creativity. The Spirit is not limited by form; it uses whatever you are willing to offer as a channel. Your daily life is filled with other potential supports: a dedicated music playlist, a particular garment, a fragrance that evokes your future, or even a daily walking ritual. The only true rule is resonance. The best support is the one that captures your attention and causes your inner certainty to vibrate.

Unity in diversity. You are free to choose your own path. For some, a single support—such as a vision notebook kept with disciplined consistency—will be enough to anchor the vision. For others, it is the combination of multiple supports that creates the ecosystem needed to saturate the mind with the promise and leave no room for doubt. Combining supports is like creating a symphony, where each instrument plays the same melody from a different angle. It is a way of surrounding your senses so that wherever your eyes fall or your hands move, the vision is recalled.

The choice is yours. Do not seek methodological perfection but sincerity of commitment. Whether you choose one tool or a complete set, the essence remains the same: to keep your attention alive until the vision becomes self-evident. Like the stars for Abraham, these supports exist only to remind you of what is already in motion.

5.2. Unshakable Faith as the Key to Manifestation

Between the dream and its fulfillment, there is an invisible force that determines whether your project will remain an idea or become a reality: unshakable faith.

Faith is not a vague belief or a fragile hope. It is a deep conviction, an inner certainty that refuses doubt and acts as a creative engine. Without it, intention remains a thought, vision stays an image, and goals are nothing more than words. With it, everything you carry in your mind is transformed into a living energy that attracts, aligns, and materializes.

Unshakable faith is the power that moves you to act as if you had already received what you hope for. It is not your strategic plan alone that guarantees success but the emotional and spiritual force with which you already inhabit your future. What you live internally with intensity eventually manifests externally.

Remember this progression:

- Your intention positions you as a channel of abundance (Chapter 1)
- Your vision integrates your deepest and most authentic desires (Chapter 2)
- Your goals translate your ambition into structure and movement (Chapters 3 and 4)

All of this—abundance, desire, ambition—may seem distant or inaccessible. Yet you are called to believe and to live as if you had already received what you are pursuing. Feel it. Embody it. Walk as though it were already accomplished.

Your current environment may push you toward doubt, but you are not limited by what you see. You walk with God, who is able to give you all things—on the condition that you manifest unshakable faith. I am not asking you to deny your present situation but to build a resilient mindset and to begin defining who you are based on who you are becoming.

This is precisely why materializing your dreams on tangible supports—journals, vision boards, diagrams—is essential. These tools create a new environment around you, one that no longer reflects only your present but above all your future. They remind you daily of who you already are in the reality you are beginning to experience internally.

Dare to see and feel victory, prosperity, abundance, and peace every day. The more you nourish your mind with these images, the more they become your new identity. You are not merely dreaming—you are conditioning your entire being to live that future now. Change your language. Change your thoughts. Change your emotional posture toward your life.

You become what you consistently behold. And when you choose to behold greatness, you activate the process that inevitably leads you toward it.

Scripture defines faith as:

"Now faith is the substance of things hoped for, the evidence of things not seen."
— Hebrews 11:1

Faith is therefore not an intellectual belief but a felt and vibrant conviction. It is a deep inner assurance that causes you to walk as though what you hope for has already been received.

5.2.1. The Woman with the Issue of Blood—Faith That Seizes Victory

For twelve years, this woman suffered from an incurable flow of blood. Physicians had failed, her financial resources were exhausted, and human hope had vanished. Yet within her mind, she had rooted an absolute conviction:

"For she said to herself, 'If I only touch His garment, I will be healed.'"
— Matthew 9:21

This detail is crucial: "she said to herself."

It means that she had engraved this thought into her imagination and was repeating it continually. She was feeding her subconscious with this image—she saw it, she believed it, she felt it. She repeatedly visualized the scene: Jesus passing by, herself approaching Him, and healing bursting forth at the moment of contact.

Her imagination, emotions, and faith were already aligned with that reality. She had received her healing in her heart before receiving it in her body. Her mental and emotional preparation was so strong, her conviction so absolute, that the external manifestation became inevitable.

And when Jesus passed by, she did everything necessary to touch Him. In the midst of the crowd pressing against Him, her touch was different—it was charged with unshakable faith. Jesus perceived the release of that power:

"Someone touched Me…"

And He declared to her:

"Daughter, your faith has made you well."— Matthew 9:22

This episode reveals a universal law: what you deeply believe, what you visualize with intensity, and what you repeat internally with conviction, eventually manifests in your reality. Faith is not passive waiting—it is a creative force that seizes the promise and renders it tangible.

5.2.2. Unshakable Faith: The Absolute Condition for Manifestation

This testimony reveals a universal law: believe before you see.

True faith does not wait for visible evidence in order to act; it already lives the promise internally as fulfilled. Jesus Himself affirmed this truth:

"Blessed are those who have not seen and yet have believed." — John 20:29

Unshakable faith is therefore not an option—it is the absolute condition for manifesting your intention, your vision, and your goals. It is the firm assurance of what is hoped for, the inner evidence of what is not yet visible (Hebrews 11:1).

This is why you are called to keep your attention continually focused on what you have materialized: your vision journal, your vision board, your diagrams, or any other support you have chosen. These supports are not mere tools; they are spiritual anchors that train your mind and emotions to already live this future with intensity. Every reading, every contemplation, every repetition engraves your vision more deeply into your subconscious—until it becomes an unshakable conviction.

And once this conviction is rooted, it functions like an internal autopilot. Your thoughts, your emotions, and your actions naturally align with your objective. You no longer live in waiting but in the inner embodiment of success. And because you already live it within, external reality eventually bends to your inner state.

CHAPTER 6

ACTION: EMBODYING THE COVENANT

Introduction: From Vision to Embodiment: The Power of the Fourth Pillar

Within the movement of the four pillars we have explored, action is not the starting point—it is the sacred culmination. If intention purified your source (to intend), if strategy charted your path (to plan), and if faith released your inner power (to believe), then action is the moment when the invisible finally agrees to become matter.

To embody the covenant is to transform conviction into gesture. It is the signal sent to Heaven that you are no longer content to dream or to plan but that you are ready to receive. Without this fourth pillar, the previous three remain like clouds without rain—beautiful to contemplate but incapable of fertilizing the soil.

Action, as we approach it here, is not frantic agitation meant to "force" destiny. It is the seal of faithfulness. It is conscious cooperation with providence. By taking action—even a modest one—you offer a concrete channel to the abundance you have already called forth with your mind and your heart.

In this chapter, we will explore how to act without burning out, how to transform every task into a living prayer, and how to make your daily life the very ground where your mission takes form.

6.1. Quiet Action: Executing Your STGs and the Principle of the End

The most common mistake after the anchoring phase is inertia. Many people wait for the "perfect" opportunity, the "complete" funding, or the "ideal" resources before acting at the level of their vision. But this waiting is a trap—it places human circumstances above divine cooperation.

God, on the contrary, often tests faithfulness in modest beginnings. He does not ask your hands for the impossible but for constancy in what is already possible. This is where the concrete execution of your Short-Term Goals (STGs) begins—those small daily seeds that prepare the future harvest.

The Context of Zechariah 4:5–10

The prophet Zechariah speaks to Zerubbabel, governor of Judah, charged with rebuilding the Temple after exile. The task was immense, resources were limited, and opposition was strong. Yet God gave him this promise:

"The hands of Zerubbabel have laid the foundation of this house; his hands shall also complete it… For who has despised the day of small beginnings?"
— Zechariah 4:9–10

This passage is a call to dream big while starting small. God reminds us that the greatness of a work is not measured by its visible beginnings but by the faithfulness of the one who perseveres. "Small beginnings" are not signs of mediocrity—they are the training ground where faith is strengthened and quiet action prepares fulfillment.

The Principle of the End

To act according to the Kingdom is to walk while already carrying the end within your heart. You keep your DAP Vision (Desire, Love, Potential) and your Long-Term Goal (LTG) before you as a compass. By faith, you live them in your imagination and emotions as if the promise were already fulfilled.

At the same time, you honor the present step—the one that is available to you today. You know clearly where you are going, yet you humbly accept to begin with what is small, concrete, and accessible, trusting that every faithful step brings the invisible closer to the visible.

Each STG you execute is a stone laid on the path toward your LTG. These modest gestures—sending an email, drafting a plan, saving a sum, meeting a key person—are what, over time, build the structure of your vision.

The Secret of Faithfulness

Never despise small actions. They are like the invisible hammer strikes that shape a cathedral. God does not multiply what you wait for—He multiplies what you undertake. The greatness of your vision manifests when you honor beginnings, because faithfulness is proven in the hidden place.

Thus, the path toward your LTG inevitably passes through the disciplined execution of your STGs. Take the list of actions you established in Chapter 4 and begin checking them off, one by one. Every step—no matter how small—is a silent declaration of your faith in the final fulfillment.

Your Vision (LTG) Requires...	Your Quiet Action (STG) Begins With...
You want an international business	Start by selling to one person. Treat that first client like a major account.
You want to lead a large team	Start by managing one project with excellence. Manage your own time and finances with discipline.
You want doors to open	Start by knocking. Send the email. Make the call. Take the course.
You dream of a published book	Start by writing the first paragraph—or even just the detailed outline of chapter one.

The Language of Faith: A Signal to Heaven

Every small action you take, every Short-Term Goal you begin to execute, is never insignificant. In the eyes of Heaven, it is a silent yet powerful declaration: "I am ready for what comes next." Your daily actions become living evidence of your maturity and determination.

These first steps are not mere administrative tasks or practical details. They are the language of your faith—the dialect through which your heart speaks to God and to the world. Every action taken despite an apparent lack of resources is a proclamation: "I believe the vision will be fulfilled, and I choose to move forward."

When you act faithfully in what is small, you activate the principle of divine cooperation. You have done your part—you have planted. And by planting, you demonstrate that you are ready for the multiplication He has promised—for it is God who waters and makes things grow.

Quiet action is the expression of a faith that refuses to remain abstract. It is the proof that you will not stay in theory. It is the seal that distinguishes those who speak about abundance from those who actually walk in abundance.

Every STG you execute is like a stone placed in the construction of your future. It is a seed that cries out to Heaven:

"Lord, I believe in Your promise—and I make it visible through my hands."

And Heaven always responds to this language, for faith without works is dead—but faith expressed through action becomes unstoppable.

6.2. The Principle of Divine Cooperation: Sowing for the Harvest

You are not called to carry the weight of your destiny alone but to live it in cooperation with divine power. Scripture establishes a clear distinction of responsibilities: man sows, and God makes things grow. This is the immutable law of the seed—a law that transcends generations and cannot be annulled.

Remember this: your vision and your goals are so expansive that they awaken in you both awe and conviction. That tension is the sign that you are on the right path. For if you could accomplish everything by your own strength, without God's help, your goal would be too small—too human. But when your vision leads you to say, "Lord, without You this is impossible. But with You, all things are possible," then you are exactly where you need to be: in the territory of faith, where human action meets divine multiplication.

Greatness That Requires Faith

An authentic vision is always larger than your current means. It forces you out of the logic of control and into the logic of divine dependence. It uproots self-sufficiency and anchors you in heavenly provision. In this way, God ensures that your success will not merely be the product of your talents but a testimony of His grace.

The Human Part and the Divine Part

Your faith must now take the form of action. You are called to do what is possible at your level: take concrete steps, execute your Short-Term Goals (STGs), and plant visible seeds. It is through this practical obedience that you encounter the grace of God—because He alone accomplishes what lies beyond your power.

God never causes to grow what has not been sown. He does not multiply emptiness but what you place in His hands. Your role is to plant faithfully; His role is to bring forth growth and fruit. You must therefore commit first to doing what is within your reach, and God will support your obedience by opening the windows of heaven.

Divine cooperation is not the abandonment of responsibility—it is an alliance: you do what is possible, and God does what is impossible. You sow in the field of your daily life, and He sends the rain, the sunlight, and the increase. You lay the stone, and He builds the structure. You extend your hand, and He opens the doors.

God's Invisible Architecture: When Heaven Orchestrates your Steps

To illustrate how Heaven responds to a clear intention, sustained attention, and committed action, allow me to share a personal experience that remains for me a living testimony of divine orchestration.

In December 2012, while I was serving as a Program Coordinator for an international organization in Farchana, eastern Chad—where we were working to support the education of Sudanese refugee children and youth—I set my Short-Term Goals (STGs) for the coming year. Among them was a precise professional objective:

"To develop a level of professional English sufficient to function effectively in both Francophone and Anglophone contexts."

At that time, my work was conducted approximately 70% in French and 30% in English. I had made a deliberate decision to act—to improve my English—convinced that this skill would become a strategic lever for my mission.

Three months later, Providence opened an unexpected door: I was promoted to Country Director for Chad within the same organization. Suddenly, the linguistic balance reversed. My new role required 70% English and only 30% French. All my reports and remote meetings with headquarters in the United Kingdom were conducted entirely in English. My direct counterpart, the Finance Director, spoke only English. One month after this promotion, I was even required to prepare and deliver a presentation at a roundtable in Washington, D.C., where all discussions took place in English.

These new responsibilities placed me in a professional and linguistic environment that almost forced me, by the end of that year, to reach the very objective I had set. Learning and working in English was no longer an option—it became a vital necessity. What might have seemed overwhelming just months earlier became the perfect environment for the fulfillment of a goal I had clearly written down.

This experience reveals a profound truth: I had set a clear objective; I had nourished that intention with attention and effort (action); and God orchestrated the impossible by creating conditions that compelled me to rise to the level of my goal. Not only did I achieve what I had set out to do, but I also crossed a professional threshold I had not anticipated at the time.

The promotion was the unexpected bonus—but one perfectly orchestrated by the Lord to help me fulfill my original objective.

6.3. Doing Good around You: The Invisible Law That Accelerates Your Destiny

"He went around doing good." — Acts 10:38

This simple sentence summarizes the life of Jesus—but it also reveals a higher strategy for living. Jesus did not limit Himself to spectacular miracles meant for the crowds; He consistently sowed acts of kindness. In doing so, He revealed a powerful spiritual law: the good you do, without calculation, becomes a seed that works in your favor—often in unexpected ways.

Everything we have explored so far has taught you how to clarify your intention, build your vision, and take strategic action to achieve your goals. But there is another form of action—just as decisive, though often overlooked: doing good around you with a pure and selfless heart. This practice is not a detour from your destiny; it is often the fastest shortcut toward it.

6.3.1. The Unexpected Harvest of an Ordinary Gesture

I remember a moment in my life that, in hindsight, perfectly illustrates this invisible Kingdom principle: the good you do—quietly and sincerely—becomes the seed of an opportunity God prepares for you.

At the time, I was living in Abidjan. A close friend of mine, deeply engaged in academic research in history and international relations, asked me for help. He knew I was completing my studies in modern literature, and he needed a careful eye to improve syntax, lighten dense sentences, and bring greater clarity and flow to his work. His ideas were strong, but his writing was often complex, and he asked me to help restructure his arguments so the text could breathe.

I never viewed this request as a "job"—and certainly not as an opportunity. For me, it was simply an act of friendship: a gift of time, skill, and heart. I reviewed his document, corrected it, restructured it, simplified it, and clarified it—expecting nothing in return.

I had no idea that this small seed would produce a harvest.

A few months later, his work gained significant recognition from a diplomatic mission that began to solicit him regularly for consultancy work. Then one day, that same institution was seeking to recruit someone for a very specific role: drafting diplomatic correspondence, reviewing official texts, editing, and reformulating documents.

Exactly my field.
Exactly my skill set.
Exactly what I desired.

They asked my friend if he knew someone suitable. He did not hesitate for a second—he gave them my name. He connected us, I submitted my application—and I was selected.

At that moment, I was unemployed. I had just entered a new phase of my life—one in which I was beginning to set clear goals, refine my vision, and orient my professional path toward international relations. And suddenly, without actively seeking it, an opportunity appeared that aligned perfectly with my desire, my plan, and my vision.

I could never have orchestrated this myself. I could never have forced that door open. I could never have predicted such perfect timing. Today, I understand clearly what God was doing: He used my selfless gesture as a seed—a seed of service, a seed of love, a seed of excellence—and He transformed it into a connection, a recommendation, an open door, and a position—exactly where my path (as defined in Chapters 3 and 4) was leading.

This experience anchored in me a deep conviction:

Nothing you do in love is ever wasted. Every act of service becomes a seed in the soil of destiny. God uses what you do for others to open what He has prepared for you.

6.3.2. The Universal Principle: What You Release Always Returns to You

Across all traditions—biblical, spiritual, economic, and psychological—we encounter the same law:

Life responds to what you do for others.

- “A man reaps what he sows.” (Galatians 6:7)
- “Give, and it will be given to you.” (Luke 6:38)
- In psychology, this is known as the principle of reciprocity (Cialdini)

- In economics, it is the law of social capital: what you give creates invisible networks of opportunity
- In personal development, it is the law of return, the dynamic flow of giving and receiving

Life is designed in such a way that you never move forward alone. Every door that opens is held by a human hand that God has placed along your path. To do good is to plant hands that, one day, will open doors you could never have forced by yourself.

Why Generosity and Kindness Accelerate Your Destiny

They elevate your inner state (psychology and neuroscience)

Kindness activates areas of the brain associated with creativity, relational intelligence, decision-making, and perseverance. You become clearer, more inspired, and more effective. Generosity does not drain you—it sharpens you.

They expand your invisible network (sociology)

Every act of goodwill creates a witness, a memory, a loyalty, and often a future recommendation. You build social capital. Many of your greatest opportunities are hidden in relationships you have not yet encountered.

They position you as a solution, not a petitioner

The world consistently opens doors to those who bring value. When you do good, you become someone who brings peace, clarity, encouragement, support, or solutions. Your presence becomes sought after—and so do your projects.

They attract providence (spiritual law)

When you become a source, God becomes your reservoir. He sustains those who sustain others. Generosity is one of the fastest ways to invite divine intervention into your journey.

The good you do always returns—but often through a different door. The person you bless is not necessarily the one who will bless you in return. This is the principle of circulating good.

You give here.
You sow there.
You encourage elsewhere.
You help quietly.

And then—one day, when you least expect it—God sends someone else to open a door you could never have imagined.

In the Kingdom, nothing done in love is ever lost.
Everything circulates.
Everything returns.
Everything multiplies.

Why Kindness Must Become a Strategy, Not an Occasional Gesture

Because:

- Some blessings are released only when you become a source
- Some doors open only to clean and sincere hearts
- Some speeds are activated only for those who serve
- Some destinies are unlocked only through sustained giving

What you do for others prepares what God will do for you.

The Invisible Law of Acceleration

You accelerate your destiny when you:

- Intentionally do good
- Sow into someone's life
- Support the work of God
- Become a source of light
- Multiply peace around you
- Offer your talent, your network, or your resources
- Encourage someone who was about to give up

Because in the Kingdom:

- Kindness is speed
- Service is strategy
- Love is a shortcut
- Destiny responds not to competition but to contribution

Stories — When Kindness Changes a Destiny

The Man Who Paid for a Taxi… and Became a Millionaire

A few years ago, a man named James, a young entrepreneur in Lagos, was leaving a conference late at night. Outside the venue, he noticed a student stranded with no money, unable to get home. Without hesitation, James paid for the young man's taxi fare. The amount was insignificant.

Deeply touched, the student said, "One day, I'll repay you."

James waved it off gently and replied, "Just help someone else when you can."

Ten years later, James was desperately seeking an investor to launch a mobile payment platform. Exhausted and close to giving up, he found himself pitching before an investment committee. Midway through the presentation, the chairman interrupted him and said:

"I know you. You're the man who paid for my taxi ten years ago. Today, it's my turn to open a door for you."

The result: a one-million-dollar investment.

A simple act—returned through a different door.

The Teacher Who Changed the Destiny of a Poor Child.

In 1992, a schoolteacher in Kinshasa noticed a bright student who arrived hungry every morning. Quietly, without drawing attention, she began bringing him a small bread roll during every break.

That child was Dr. Denis Mukwege, future Nobel Peace Prize laureate.

In his memoirs, he dedicates an entire chapter to her and writes: "She did not feed my stomach. She fed my destiny."

Kindness is never small.

The Taxi Driver Who Helped a Stranger… Who Was Not a Stranger.

In Abidjan, a taxi driver named Gervais encountered a man struggling to withdraw money from an ATM. The man needed to get to the airport urgently. Trusting him, Gervais drove him without payment.

That traveler turned out to be a senior executive at a major telecommunications company.

Two weeks later, the man summoned Gervais to the company headquarters and offered him an exclusive contract to transport company executives.

Within eighteen months, Gervais went from renting a single taxi to owning a small fleet of vehicles.

Because kindness opens doors that diplomas cannot.

These stories are not isolated miracles. They reveal a law:

When an act of kindness leaves your heart, a door opens somewhere in the world.

You don't know when.
You don't know where.
But God knows exactly how to multiply the seeds you plant in secret.

Doing good around you is not weakness.
It is a strategy of elevation.
It is acceleration.
It is a law of the Kingdom.

6.3.3. The Tithe: Aligning the Heart with the Source of Abundance

In the pursuit of prosperity without losing one's soul, the tithe is neither a religious tax nor a mere financial rule. It is a prophetic act by which we declare that God is the true Owner of everything we possess. It is an act of alignment that transforms income into a seed of blessing.

God Is the Source; Your Work Is Only a Channel

To build lasting abundance without spiritual compromise, it is essential not to confuse the source with the channel. One of the greatest illusions of the modern world is the belief that our security depends on our job, our clients, or the state of the market.

There is a vital distinction:

God is your only Source. Your work, investments, or business are merely channels—paths through which He collaborates with you to release His provision.

Why does this distinction change everything?

- If your work is your source, your peace is fragile. You live in constant fear: *If I lose this job, I lose everything.*
- If God is your source, when a channel closes (layoff, crisis, lost contract), you do not panic. You know the Owner of the river can open another channel—wider and deeper—to reach you.

The Apostle Paul stated this with absolute certainty:

"And my God will supply all your needs according to His riches in glory in Christ Jesus."
— Philippians 4:19

He did not say your employer will provide—he said **my God**.

Trusting money is building on sand.
Trusting God is standing on the Rock of Ages.

This is where the tithe finds its true meaning: it tests where your security lies. By returning to God what already belongs to Him, you declare:

"Lord, I acknowledge that it is not this job that sustains me—it is You."

An Alliance of Gratitude—Long Before the Law

Long before commandments were engraved in stone, the tithe was already the language of gratitude. When Abraham returned victorious, he gave a tenth of everything to Melchizedek (Genesis 14:20), acknowledging that his success came from the Most High.

Later, in the wilderness, Jacob made this vow:

"Of all that You give me, I will give You a tenth." — Genesis 28:22

From its very origin, the tithe is the response of a heart overwhelmed by divine provision.

A Portion Consecrated to the Lord

Scripture reminds us that the tithe is not something we give to God—it already belongs to Him:

"A tithe of everything from the land… belongs to the Lord; it is holy to the Lord." — Leviticus 27:30

By setting aside the first ten percent, we honor the principle of priority:

"Honor the Lord with your wealth, with the first fruits of all your income." — Proverbs 3:9–10

Then our barns are filled—not by effort alone but by the favor that accompanies obedience.

The Engine of Vision and Solidarity

God instituted the tithe so that His house would lack nothing and His work would advance. It sustains those dedicated to divine service (Numbers 18:21) and ensures the church remains a functional lighthouse within society (Nehemiah 10:37–38).

But the tithe also carries a profound social dimension: it is meant to support the foreigner, the orphan, and the widow (Deuteronomy 14:28–29).

To prosper without losing one's soul is to understand that your surplus is often the answer to someone else's distress.

The Invitation to the Divine Challenge

Malachi 3:10 resounds as the only promise in Scripture where God explicitly invites us to put Him to the test. By bringing the tithe, we open the "windows of heaven." This is where faith meets finance: we stop relying on our own calculations and enter into the arithmetic of grace.

The Spirit Beyond the Letter

For the conscious builder, Jesus brings a crucial clarification in Matthew 23:23: the tithe must never be practiced at the expense of justice, mercy, and faithfulness. Giving does not exempt us from cultivating a pure heart. As the Epistle to the Hebrews explains (Hebrews 7:1–9), the principle of the tithe transcends historical periods and connects us to an eternal priesthood.

By practicing the tithe, you do not impoverish your bank account—you deepen your connection to the Source.

You do not give in order to receive; you give because you have already received the greatest wealth of all: the presence of God within your projects.

6.3.4. Providence in Motion: When Synchronicities Confirm Alignment

When you begin to apply the principles of this book, you will notice a remarkable phenomenon. Events that the world labels as "coincidences" or "luck" will start multiplying in your daily life.

In psychology, this is called synchronicity: the simultaneous occurrence of two events with no direct causal link, yet carrying deep meaning for the one who experiences them. For the conscious builder, we call this **providence.**

The Sign That You Are on God's Frequency

Synchronicity is the language through which the Creator responds. It is the phone call that comes at the exact moment you were formulating a need, or the "chance" encounter in an airport that unlocks a project you had been struggling with for months.

These signs are not accidents. They are evidence of divine cooperation and grace. As Proverbs 16:9 reminds us:

"In their hearts humans plan their course, but the Lord establishes their steps."

Synchronicity is the Lord establishing your steps in a visible way.

Alignment as a Magnet for Opportunities

Why do these signs appear now? Because by following these three pillars, you have created the conditions for reception:

Through Intention – You have aligned your heart and your life with God's perspective on abundance. You have declared to the Source of all provision that you are now willing to be His channel—to bless others and glorify His name. Providence never forces doors closed by selfishness, but it opens wide those unlocked by clarity and altruism. By recognizing God as your only Source (and not your job, clients, or market), you have released anxiety. This release creates the necessary space—the sacred vacuum—into which Providence can finally move and act.

Through Attention – You have disciplined your inner gaze. You stopped feeding fear, urgency, and distraction, and deliberately chose to cultivate faith. By materializing your vision and goals on tangible supports, revisiting them regularly, and consecrating them through prayer accompanied by thanksgiving, you have anchored within yourself a stable inner image of your fulfilled vision. Your fully focused attention makes your mind receptive, available, and aligned. You discern opportunities more clearly, recognize the right encounters, and perceive the right timing. Your perception is now calibrated to recognize providence. Where attention is focused, providence becomes legible.

Through Action – You began to move. Providence accompanies motion; it does not precede immobility. Through the good you do around you and through the practice of the tithe, you activate the law of divine circulation. There is a connection that goes beyond human reasoning, intelligence, and logic, yet is deeply real—between generosity and the emergence of synchronicities. By practicing the tithe, you declare that money is not your master but your servant. This act releases a dynamic of constant flow: by being faithful in managing what is small, you open the channel for unexpected resources—often far greater than the tithe itself—to reach you through paths your logic could never have designed. God becomes your business partner, and His ability to open doors infinitely surpasses human calculations.

Learning to Read and Cultivate Divine "Winks"

Once your inner gaze has been calibrated through focused attention, providence no longer merely acts—it begins to dialogue with you. Synchronicities then become a language: subtle yet precise "winks" through which God confirms your alignment and encourages you to keep going.

However, these signs only bear fruit if you learn to recognize them, honor them, and respond to them. Providence never imposes itself; it reveals itself to those who develop active attention.

Recognizing the Signs

Begin by observing and noting those moments when "everything fell perfectly into place": a timely encounter, a piece of information received at the exact moment you needed it, a solution that appeared without visible effort. By consciously acknowledging these moments, you sharpen your spiritual discernment. What you recognize gains clarity; what you ignore fades. The more attentive you become to these signs, the more frequently they appear.

Gratitude as a Spiritual Amplifier

Each time you say—silently or aloud—"Thank You, Lord, for this coincidence," you are doing more than expressing thanks. You are strengthening the covenant. Gratitude is a powerful key: it opens the channel and widens the flow. What you thank God for continues. What you honor multiplies. Gratitude transforms an isolated event into a lasting dynamic.

The Courage of the Moment

Finally, providence calls for a response. When a synchronicity appears—a sudden idea, an unexpected invitation, a person encountered "by chance"—do not wait too long. Grace opens the door, but it is up to you to walk through it. Immediate action seals the cooperation. Faith recognizes the sign; courage embodies it. Providence always accompanies movement. It confirms steps already taken, never immobility.

Synchronicities are God's gentle kisses on your aligned efforts. They do not replace discipline or action, but they confirm them. They remind you that you are no longer moving alone or against the current. You are no longer striving blindly to succeed—you are succeeding because you have entered into harmony with the river of life, and that river knows exactly where it is going.

6.3.5. The Power of Gratitude: Your Accelerator of Abundance

If intention is the seed and action the watering, gratitude is the sun that ripens the harvest. For you, the conscious builder, gratitude is not a polite formula—it is a spiritual force of attraction. It is the signal you send to the Source saying: "I recognize Your hand, and I am ready for what comes next."

Gratitude Secures Your Inner Peace

The world chases success in constant fear of lack, producing tension and inner unrest. Gratitude, on the other hand, rests on the certainty of divine provision. The Apostle Paul gives us the key in Philippians 4:6:

"Do not be anxious about anything, but in everything, by prayer and supplication, with thanksgiving, present your requests to God."

Notice the order: thanksgiving accompanies the request. By thanking God before seeing the outcome, you affirm your faith. This posture of the heart drives out anxiety, which would otherwise suffocate your projects and steal your joy.

The Secret of Multiplication

There is a foundational principle you must grasp: what you give thanks for multiplies. We see this clearly in the miracle of the loaves (John 6:11). Jesus did not complain about having only five loaves and two fish for a massive crowd. He took what was available, gave thanks, and that act of gratitude opened the door to the miracle.

In your business or finances, thanking God for the "small"—that first modest contract, that initial savings, that emerging idea—is the trigger for future abundance. If you cannot be grateful for small victories, you will not be able to steward greater ones without losing your soul.

Gratitude Turns Your Attention into a Magnet for Favor

The psalmist declares:

"Enter His gates with thanksgiving and His courts with praise." — Psalm 100:4

Gratitude is the key that opens the doors to divine opportunities.

A grateful heart is an open heart; a complaining heart closes in on itself. Complaint isolates you and blinds you to synchronicities. Gratitude, by contrast, sharpens your attention. It allows you to see grace where others see only chance. It creates an atmosphere of peace around you that naturally attracts the right partners and unexpected favor.

Your Shield Against Pride

Finally, gratitude is the anchor that prevents your soul from drifting into the arrogance of the "self-made" mindset. By saying thank you, you remember that:

"Every good and perfect gift comes from above, from the Father of lights." — James 1:17

Gratitude keeps you humble, reminding you that while you may be the channel, He remains the Source. This is how you can possess wealth without letting wealth possess you.

The Law of Circulation: Gratitude and Abundance

Foundational Principle: What circulates amplifies. What stagnates dries up.

1. Gratitude Opens the Flow

Gratitude is not a passive emotion—it is an act of spiritual recognition. When you give thanks sincerely:

- You acknowledge the Source (God, Life) as the origin of what you receive
- You affirm that what is already present is sufficient to act
- You shift from a mindset of lack to a posture of reception

Spiritually, gratitude declares: **"I see. I recognize. I trust."**

It is not denial of effort—it is recognition of grace.

2. Abundance Responds to Recognition

Abundance is not limited to material wealth. It includes:

- Opportunities
- Meaningful encounters
- Inspired ideas

- Right timing (synchronicities/providence)

When gratitude becomes consistent, abundance circulates more freely because it is no longer blocked by:

- Complaint
- Comparison
- Fear of lack

Gratitude clears the channel. It signals that the heart is open, aligned, and capable of stewarding more.

3. The Trap: Receiving Without Gratitude

Receiving without gratitude creates a break in circulation:

- Abundance becomes heavy
- It generates attachment, fear, or arrogance
- It eventually stagnates or withdraws

This is not punishment. It is a law of spiritual coherence.

What is not acknowledged cannot remain in healthy circulation.

4. The Virtuous Cycle

You receive → You give thanks → You act with what you have → The flow intensifies → You receive more → Your gratitude deepens.

This is how visible providence is born.

Abundance does not increase because of accumulation but because of circulation.

5. A Practical Key for Integration

Each day, ask yourself one simple question:

“What did I receive today that I could not have produced by my own efforts alone?”

Then give thanks. Even briefly. Even silently.

Gratitude is the spiritual currency that keeps abundance in motion.

What you thank God for remains. What you honor grows.

CONCLUSION

THE SENDING FORTH

You have reached the end of this book, yet in truth, you are standing at the threshold of your true expansion.

What you are closing here is not just another teaching—it is a passage. What you have read was not meant merely to be understood but to be embodied.

You now know that abundance is not a struggle but an alignment. It is not an external conquest wrested from the world but an inner circulation that one allows.

It is not a destination to be reached but the natural consequence of a unified being—aligned in intention, clear in vision, faithful in belief, and coherent in action.

If you have done the exercises, if you have taken the time to look inward with honesty, something has already shifted. Perhaps not yet in your numbers, but in your perspective. And that inner shift is always the first miracle.

You have learned that prosperity which brings peace begins at the source: in what you truly desire, in why you desire it, and in the way you choose to walk toward it.

You Now Hold the Four Keys of Your Covenant

To Intend (Intention)

Your intention has been purified. You no longer desire to fill a void or to prove your worth, but to manifest a mission. Your intention is no longer an inner tension but a clear direction. The source has been restored.

To Plan (Strategy)

Your strategy has given form to your aspirations. By structuring your vision and setting clear, ordered goals, you have prepared a channel through which grace can flow without confusion. You no longer control out of fear; you plan out of wisdom.

To Believe (Faith)

Your faith has changed in nature. It is no longer a fragile hope suspended from circumstances but a discipline of attention. You have learned to nourish what you want to see grow, to fix your gaze on the promise rather than the obstacle, to inhabit victory inwardly before it becomes visible. Your faith has become stable, active, and deeply rooted.

To Embody (Action)

Your action is now your seal. With every faithful step—no matter how modest—you declare to Heaven that you are ready. You no longer act alone, nor against life, nor in agitation. You cooperate with Providence. And where action aligns, heaven responds.

From This Moment Forward

From this moment forward, your role is clear:

Walk with certainty.
Plan with wisdom.
Act with courage.
But above all—believe with boldness.

Give thanks at every stage, for gratitude is the breath that widens the flow. What you give thanks for is strengthened. What you acknowledge multiplies. Gratitude keeps you in the right posture: that of the conscious builder—neither arrogant nor anxious, but grounded in trust.

Also observe what will begin to unfold along your path. As your alignment stabilizes, you will notice openings, encounters, sudden ideas, and impeccable timing. The world will call these coincidences. You will recognize them as Providence—not magic, but a living collaboration between your faithfulness and divine wisdom.

Remember this: **you are not called to force reality but to meet it with rightness.** When intention is pure, vision is clear, faith is cultivated, and action is faithful, the river widens on its own.

Now Look at That River

Now look at that river.

It is not born of fear but of alignment.
It does not impose itself; it flows.
And it flows through you.

You are no longer a mere spectator of your life. You have become a conscious builder, an inspired creator, a faithful channel of abundance.

Go now. Live what you have understood. Embody what you believe. And let your prosperity testify—not to your ego, but to the just order that emerges when soul, action, and faith walk together.

The book closes.

The work begins.

ABOUT THE AUTHOR

Kevin Adou is a consultant, strategist, and trainer.

He supports leaders, entrepreneurs, and organizations in building success that is aligned—integrating faith, strategy, and sustainable impact. At the crossroads of personal development, biblical wisdom, and practical action, he is committed to promoting a form of prosperity that elevates without compromising integrity or inner peace.

www.ingramcontent.com/pod-product-compliance
Lightning Source LLC
LaVergne TN
LVHW010946110826
845149LV00015B/3231